The 5th Space gives important recog
working with and building effectiv
young people. What has long been
standardize in organizational approa
leadership—the 5th Space clears up cobwebs and gives you simple, effective, and concise ways of understanding what empowering young people is really all about. We found it extremely helpful in deepening our thought process and how we develop, monitor, and evaluate youth-led leadership, both from a qualitative and quantitative perspective.

Ishita Chaudhary
Founder and CEO of The
YP Foundation (TYPF) and
Change Looms, Pravah
alumnus, New Delhi

This book is a must read. This is a significant contribution from sensitive life-crafters. More than a book, it brings to life the essentials of the 5th Space-generated youth leadership. This space truly defines us, refines us, enlarges us.... Allows us to debunk, uncover, and discover ourselves. Frees ourselves. Freeing is creating, creating is crafting, crafting is carving, carving is chiseling, chiseling is churning, churning is elevating–enlivening–caring. A self-exploration that is the key to any transformation—whether in the Self or the Society. Youth for youth: of themselves, for themselves, by themselves.

Indu Prakash Singh
Head, Urban Poverty,
CityMakers Programme,
Indo Global Social Service
Society, New Delhi

It's very central that every young person should be given the opportunity to explore themselves and their potential to be contributors to their fellow human beings, other young people, the communities they live in, and society around them. And in doing that they not just become active and connected citizens but they also become leaders and develop all sorts of other qualities which will suit them for the rest of their lives.

There are so many young people who have been able to take the lead and do things. If we don't adopt this approach (of the 5th Space), we get bored people who are disengaged and if we do, we get young people flowering through what they do.

Michael Norton, OBE
Founder of Changemakers,
YouthBank and UnLtd, UK

Every individual needs to go through this journey. We have been listening for too long to others and what they think is right for us. We have never been allowed to ask questions and decide for ourselves about what we should do. The 5th Space gives us a wonderful opportunity to know who we are and to become change makers—whether at office, at home, or in society.

Bidhan Chandra Singh
Planning Advisor, Greenpeace
India and SMILE Pravah
alumnus, New Delhi

With love
Kamini
Pravah + CYC

ARJUN ashraf_arjun@gmail.com

THE OCEAN IN A DROP

THE OCEAN IN A DROP

INSIDE-OUT YOUTH LEADERSHIP

Ashraf Patel, Meenu Venkateswaran, Kamini Prakash, and Arjun Shekhar for Pravah in collaboration with Commutiny—The Youth Collective and Oxfam India

www.sagepublications.com
Los Angeles • London • New Delhi • Singapore • Washington DC

Pravah in collaboration with Commutiny—The Youth Collective and Oxfam India

Jointly published in 2013 by

SAGE Publications India Pvt Ltd
B1/I-1 Mohan Cooperative Industrial Area
Mathura Road, New Delhi 110 044, India
www.sagepub.in

SAGE Publications Inc
2455 Teller Road
Thousand Oaks, California 91320, USA

SAGE Publications Ltd
1 Oliver's Yard, 55 City Road
London EC1Y 1SP, United Kingdom

SAGE Publications Asia-Pacific Pte Ltd
33 Pekin Street
#02-01 Far East Square
Singapore 048763

Published by Vivek Mehra for SAGE Publications India Pvt Ltd, typeset in 10/12 Minion by Tantla Composition Pvt Ltd, Chandigarh, and printed at Saurabh Printers Pvt Ltd.

Library of Congress Cataloging-in-Publication Data Available

ISBN: 978-81-321-0963-1 (PB)

The SAGE Team: Sharel Simon, Shreya Chakraborti, Rajib Chatterjee, and Dally Verghese

For Pravah,
the flow that became a confluence for our passion and profession,
that cleansed us of all our notions of what an organization is or should be,
as we tread the thin line between a cause and a joyful community,
the flow that brought the world to our feet and swept us off ours,
the flow we all chose to enter....
but hey, when did it flow into us?

Thank you for choosing a SAGE product! If you have any comment, observation or feedback, I would like to personally hear from you. Please write to me at contactceo@sagepub.in

—Vivek Mehra, Managing Director and CEO,
SAGE Publications India Pvt Ltd, New Delhi

Bulk Sales

SAGE India offers special discounts for purchase of books in bulk. We also make available special imprints and excerpts from our books on demand.

For orders and enquiries, write to us at

Marketing Department
SAGE Publications India Pvt Ltd
B1/I-1, Mohan Cooperative Industrial Area
Mathura Road, Post Bag 7
New Delhi 110044, India
E-mail us at marketing@sagepub.in

Get to know more about SAGE, be invited to SAGE events, get on our mailing list. Write today to marketing@sagepub.in

This book is also available as an e-book.

Contents

List of Illustrations ix

List of Annexures xiii

Foreword by Rashmi Bansal xv

Acknowledgments xvii

Prologue: The Classroom Is My World xix

Chapter 1 Is Society Hanging on to an Archaic Concept of the Classroom? Can Adults Really "Teach" Young People? 1

Chapter 2 If You Approach the Ocean with a Spoon, Won't It Look Like a Drop? 14

Chapter 3 What Are the Different Lenses for Viewing Youth? 32

Chapter 4 Why Are Youth-centric Spaces So Critical? 58

Chapter 5 What Design Principles Can Help to Co-create a Vibrant 5th Space? 89

Epilogue: The World Is My Classroom 127

Annexures 129

Bibliography 175

Index 178

About the Authors 183

List of Illustrations

FIGURES

2.1	We Are So Self-absorbed, Yet So Suicidal	15
2.2	Who Is Championing Youth Causes?	21
2.3	G20 Meet	23
2.4	Ex Minister of Youth Affairs Proving His Credentials	25
3.1	How Clear Are Our Views of Youth?	33
3.2	Panacea for All Evils	35
3.3	Youth *for* Development	44
3.4	Youth-centric Development	45
4.1	Youth in Search of Hangout Spaces	59
4.2	The 1st Space—The Family	60
4.3	The 2nd Space—Careers and Career-based Education	61
4.4	The 3rd Space—Leisure and Lifestyle	62
4.5	The 4th Space—Friends	64
4.6	The 5th Space: Self to Society	65
4.7	A "5th Space" during the Forties	70
4.8	The 5th Space Today ... in the Margins	82
4.9	The 5th Space: Making the Other Four Count Too	84
5.1	The SMILE Hourglass: A Youth-centric Development Process	106
5.2	Inward Bound	107
5.3	Youth Adda	108
5.4	Get Real: A Deep Self-awareness Workshop	111
5.5	SMILE In-turn-ships	114
5.6	Group Exposures	115
5.7	A Poster for the SMILE Internship Journey	117
5.8	5th Space Voyages: All Are Welcome Aboard	120
5.9	A Possible 5th Space in a BPO	122

5.10 The Need for Genuine Youth Involvement in Policymaking 124
5.11 Ministry of Youth Affairs—A Cross-cutting Ministry 125
A7.1 Iceberg Model 163
A7.2 The Explorer Funnel 165

BOXES

2.1 Youth Theories and Significant Takeaways for the Youth Sector 26
3.1 PUKAR, Mumbai 47
3.2 The YP Foundtion, New Delhi 48
3.3 Doosra Dashak, Rajasthan 49
3.4 The Bosco Institute, Guwahati 50
3.5 YUVA, Mumbai 51
3.6 SAHER, Mumbai 51
3.7 Yuv Shakti, Ahmedabad 52
3.8 Thoughtshop Foundation, Kolkata 52
3.9 Patang, Sambalpur 54
3.10 Manzil, New Delhi 55
4.1 Excerpt from "Youth and the Entertainment Mall: A Study of Prasad's Imax in Hyderabad" 62
4.2 Electronic Media in the 3rd Space 63
4.3 Cross-border Friendships 64
4.4 Youth Responses to the Bengal Famine 68
4.5 Student Action during Communal Riots, 1946 70
4.6 Myriad Ways Young People Engaged in Social Action in the Forties 72
4.7 "Your Exams and You" 74
5.1 The Making of a "Human" Engineer 93
5.2 Developing an Impact Assessment Framework for Youth Interventions 101
5.3 Exploring My Vyaktitva 112
5.4 SMILE Internship Locations (2010–2011) 115
5.5 The April 6 Youth Movement, Egypt 119
5.6 Creative Media and Policy Group 123

TABLES

2.1 Age-wise Representation in the Lok Sabha 20
2.2 Youngest Nation, Oldest Cabinet 23

List of Annexures

1	Contours of the Study	129
2	List of Key Informants	131
3	Oral Transcripts of Youth in the Forties Who Engaged in Social Action	133
4	List of Octogenarians Interviewed	147
5	Findings of the Study	149
6	Competencies and Indicators for Impact Assessment of Youth Interventions	155
7	The Vyaktitva Explorer	163

Foreword

India is a very "young country," they say. Fifty-four percent of our population is below the age of 25, and the rest is trying to look that way.

But the balance of power still lies with old people; whether in politics or business or in ordinary homes; age and position still command authority. And that, we believe, is "Indian culture."

However, the fact is you are young only once. And your mind is full of doubts and questions. This is, in fact, a good thing for society. A stone thrown into a stagnant pond creates ripples. But our ponds are too sacred to throw any kind of "stone" into them. We expect young people to simply accept *this* is what it means to be an Indian.

Without the power of discovery or deeply felt experience.

At our homes, in our schools and colleges and even at the workplace, we demand and get obedience. Then, we lament the lack of passion in our young people—their pursuit of narrow, material goals at any cost.

But who has created this monster, if not society itself?

It is in this context that this book assumes importance. Not only does it analyze the problem, it puts forth a solution. Speaking from their long experience with Pravah—a youth development nongovernmental organization (NGO), the authors put forth the idea of the "5th Space." A space where young people can engage in deep self-exploration and "Active Citizenship," going far beyond merely casting a vote.

Unfortunately this critical space is not socially legitimized unlike the other four spaces in a young person's life—the family, education and career, friends, and leisure.

This was not always so. The authors, through their research, suggest that the Independence struggle was a 5th Space in itself, and so were various student-led movements of the seventies. There is once again an opportunity to create and nurture this space, but keeping in mind the hopes and dreams of young people today.

This book argues that today we need a youth-friendly, youth-led 5th Space that nurtures youth leadership. To be successful, such a space must be co-created in partnership with young people; however, you also need trained and nonjudgmental facilitators to support them in this endeavor.

Several programs including Pravah and Manzil have used this model successfully. But we need many, many more to reach out to our vast young population.

To bring fresh ideas and energy into the idea of India.

To create a band of hungry and foolish young leaders who feel a sense of duty and devotion to the nation.

And are willing to commit themselves to "make things happen." Taking the best of the old, the best of the new, to create the best possible tomorrow for us all.

Rashmi Bansal
Mumbai, August 2012

Acknowledgments

The major insights in this book have been gained through our own experiments with youth (both the Pravah alumni and our staff). We would like to salute their openness, energy, and the sincerity they have brought to the process. They came, they saw, and they got uncomfortable.

We also owe a great debt to their parents and educators who have given them and us the space to experiment in their lives.

Partners like Commutiny—The Youth Collective, The Sir Ratan Tata Trust, and Oxfam India have been great allies in a myriad of ways: strategic*ally*, financi*ally*, intellectu*ally*, and emotion*ally*.

And how can we forget the amazing octogenarians we met while researching this publication, each of whom had a fascinating story to share; they have inspired us more than they will ever know.

Prologue
The Classroom Is My World

Ever since the India growth story has captured the middle-class imagination, we frequently overhear conversations that go something like this:

The mobile rings. "Where are you?" a male voice asks.

She answers, "Where else? You ask the same question every day."

"I keep hoping I'll get a different answer. So, on your way to class?"

"School in the morning and medical coaching classes in the evening. From one classroom to another. That's all I seem to do; as if my world is limited to the classroom."

"Break out of the prison today! There's this new hangout—something called a Youth Adda near the Khamekha Mall. I read about it in the Friday *Times*. Remember Avinash? He's from your school, that good-looking guy. Two, three years senior to you. He's showing a documentary film on Kabir. Supposed to be a great film; I read somewhere that it helps you think about yourself and all that. Also, we can talk to the facilitator about that organic food stall you wanted to run at your school fest."

"I do really want to learn more about how pesticides and chemical fertilizers harm our health. Nobody in school seems to know enough about it. Even the teachers tell me to look it up on the net. We made the right noises—'save the environment' campaigns and so on—but it's mostly second-hand knowledge. One would think that students interested in a medical career would have to know all about food produced without unhealthy pesticides. But no, they just go on studying about disease."

"What do you expect? A doc's job is only to cure."

"Why? Prevention is not a doctor's headache?"

"Ah prevention! I read that this group which has started the Youth Adda I was telling you about believes a lot in it. Prevention is their preferred approach even for social diseases like poverty."

"Huh? The only way I know how to prevent poverty is to get a fat salary as a doctor in a super specialty hospital. For which I have to pass the medical exams. Which is why I don't think it's a good idea to go to this

Youth Adda today; so please don't try to *prevent* me from going to my class."

"Else you will end up as a poor nurse...."

"Like Mom! Ya, it's her most abiding fear ... which is why you know she doesn't like me missing classes and coming home late."

"True, she is so keen to see you become a doctor. She will be devastated if you don't get through."

"I worry about that too. Everyone else in my coaching class is so super serious. No one would ever think of skipping a class for something ... so ... frivolous as an evening at a Youth Adda."

A long pause. Then, "... so I guess I'll pick you up after your coaching class at seven and take you home ... as usual."

[To be continued....]

1

Is Society Hanging on to an Archaic Concept of the Classroom? Can Adults Really "Teach" Young People?

There are now no elders who know more than the young themselves about what young people are experiencing.
Margaret Mead in *Culture and Commitment: A Study of the Generation Gap* (cited in Postman 1994, p. 89)

Margaret Mead, writing in the sixties, argued that the generation gap had widened considerably because the youth of that era were experiencing a life very different than that of the generation before. Margaret Mead's statement was an attempt to interpret the behavior of rebellious youngsters during the sixties and early seventies in the West. Those days, a million mutinies raged in homes and schools and on the streets.

Now those youngsters are grown up adults, the baby boomers as they are called, and considering how they had been "misunderstood" by their elders, one would have thought they would be careful about how to treat their young. But sadly, Margaret Mead's statement rings even more true for the new millennium: *there are now no elders who know more than the young themselves about what young people are experiencing*. Adults are again clueless about the real origins of the million mutinies raging in every part of the globe as youth aspirations spill out on the streets and clash with the existing superstructures of human civilization.

But this time the generation gap is curiously one-sided. While adults don't know what youth are experiencing, young people have never before in history been so aware of the world of adults as they are today. Due to the massive watershed in communication technology (TV and the Internet), the knowledge monopoly, once kept under lock and key by adults, is now as accessible to the young.

Adults and youth may still focus their attention on different experiences and might get excited by different things, but the knowledge gap between them has all but disappeared. As a result, echoing Neil Postman (from his book *Disappearance of Childhood*), we ask: Is youthhood itself disappearing? Was the difference between adults and young people a result of denying knowledge of the adult world to the young except in prescribed doses through the school and college funnel? As a consequence the concept of a stage called youthhood in human psychological development is under threat. Actions of young people are becoming more adult-like. For example, adolescent games are now all about playing at becoming adults—office–office, fashion cat walk, doctor–doctor, teacher–teacher. When they play traditional games like hockey, cricket, or badminton their games require supervision, spectators, and umpires (like adults) who determine which side is winning or losing.

Models as young as 15 years strut the cat walk in the West.

Youth consume and spend like adults.

Between 1950 and 1979 in the USA, the rate of serious crime by youth below the age of 15 years increased 110 times or 11,000 percent (Postman, 1994, p. 134).

In India the percentage of juvenile crime (below 18 years) to total crime has risen from 0.5 percent to 1.1 percent in the first decade of the millennium.

The young have ushered in revolutions with minimal adult leadership in the Middle East and Africa and brought adult-led governments to their knees with the recent anti-corruption movement in India. Maoism and other insurgencies continue to be a clear and present threat to the Indian Constitution. And finally the most telling evidence is coming from the classroom. As we said before, the teacher is no more the only source of knowledge and, thus, the relationship between the student and teacher has undergone a drastic change. This can be summed up in the response of one of the authors' 11-year-old daughter to a query about what she thought of her new class teacher: "She's alright but Google is better." Thus, we hypothesize along with Neil Postman that the concept of child/youthhood is well nigh into its last millennium.

Before going on to the profound impact of this imminent disappearance of youthhood on society and how society needs to respond to it, let's understand what this means for human civilization better by going back to a time when the differentiation between adults and young people first appeared.

WHEN DID THE IDEA OF CHILD/YOUTHHOOD FIRST COME INTO BEING?

"Childhood[1] is a social artefact, not a biological category," states Neil Postman (1994, p. xi):

> Our genes carry no clear instructions about who is and who is not a child, [youth] and the laws of survival do not require that a distinction be made between the world of an adult and the world of a child [youth].

So when did this social artifact—the concept of child/youthhood—first get created? Actually, children and youth as categories have existed for not more than 400 years in the West and for even less in India. The idea was first formulated during the Renaissance in sixteenth century Europe along with the idea of nation-states, science, and religious freedom. The sixteenth century is pivotal because it brought in a new invention—the printing press. One of the greatest paradoxes of the printing press was that it opened up secrets hitherto locked up in the minds of a few individuals (the Bible is a great example); yet at the same time, it created a whole lot of new secrets. To become privy to these secrets required individuals to be literate and be able to read the printed word.

A practice (that later acquired the name schooling) began in the sixteenth century (borrowing from the Greeks and Romans from much earlier times) to cloister children away from the real world till 16 years of age, ostensibly to prepare them for adulthood. Schools were the first to grade adult secrets and create a linear structure for opening them up to children gradually, stage by stage, supposedly when the child was "ready." In this way print gave rise to the divide between adults and children.

[1]Childhood includes people from 7 to 18 years (Postman 1994).

In contrast, during the oralism of the Middle Ages in Europe, childhood ended at the age of seven because by then children "have command of speech." In fact, there was no word to describe a "child" between the ages of 7 and 16. The word "child" was used to denote kinship. Seven was designated as the age of reason by the Catholic Church too, the age when an individual would know the difference between right and wrong. Of course, there were no schools during the Middle Ages in Europe; learning was through apprenticeship, on-the-job training.

In India during the Middle Ages, though a system of cloistering students away from the real world in ashrams, *gurukul*s, monasteries or *vihara*s was already established, it wasn't based as much on the written word like the schools of later ages. The *gurukul* system required students to stay with and learn through experiences and discourses with the guru. Education was mostly related to religion and youth were prepared to become priests. Heterodox education too existed, though only in a smattering of Jain and Buddhist schools.

Apart from these few religious cloisters, education was mostly imparted through apprenticeship, as in Europe, and youth were taught according to caste—the Kshatriyas learnt how to fight, the Brahmins learnt about religious scriptures, the Vaishyas learnt about commerce and other specific vocations while the Shudras were mostly denied any education.

In Europe in the Middle Ages, we also note that not only was there no practice of sequestering away the young from the adults but also in every day behavioral experience there was deemed to be no gap between the two. All kinds of language were freely used in front of children and youth, and they weren't shielded in any special way from violence.

Another practice of the Middle Ages in Europe points to the lack of the concept of shame and keeping secrets from young people that developed after the Renaissance. "The practice of playing with children's privy parts formed a widespread tradition ..." (Aries, cited in Postman 1994)—a practice that will get you up to 30 years in prison today. Thus, there was no concept of shame; the idea that one needed to hide something from a section of society because their minds weren't yet formed enough as yet to assimilate the experience without being affected by it adversely, did not exist.

In summary, in a nonliterate world, there were few secrets between adults and youth; the culture did not need "to provide training on how to understand itself" (ibid., p. 13).

WHAT'S THE ROLE OF COMMUNICATION TECHNOLOGY IN CREATING THE CONCEPT OF YOUTHHOOD?

With the invention of the printing press in the sixteenth century, a new symbolic environment was created which built up a vast store of secrets that was not easily accessible to everyone. As Harold Innis (cited in Postman 1994, p. 30) said, there are three kinds of effects that changes in communication technology inevitably tend to have:

1. They alter the things that are thought about.
2. They change what you think with (the character of symbols).
3. They radically modify the area in which thoughts develop.

That is to say, the very structure of human consciousness itself gets reshaped by changes in communication technology.

Let's see how this happened in the case of the printing press.

1. Print, by altering what was thought about, reshaped the nature of knowledge. By allowing it to be stored easily for the first time, knowledge monopolies were created. The access to these monopolies was based on literacy and access was limited to those who could decipher the new symbolic codes. It was this knowledge gap between readers and nonreaders, and adult and child that led to gaps in the public space for the first time.
2. Changing what we think with, that is, the way content was organized in a book, became a completely new way of organizing thought. In print, a story developed linearly with the preceding part leading up to what was coming. Gradually our thinking too became sequential, systematic, and analytical. James Joyce calls it mockingly "ABCED mindedness."
3. Also the community where these thoughts were being developed diversified radically. Suddenly a large group of individuals could be told the same things. The stored word could transcend geographies. Schools appeared as a result when text books and curricula could become replicable and standardized.

The school was, therefore, a product of the printing press and it soon became a space for "preparation for adulthood" (ibid., pp. 56–60).

And obviously this future-orientedness of a school came at the cost of the Now of the child. We don't say this lightly. Consider this: Print represses the natural energies of children because it requires them to sit still in a disciplined manner, curbing their instincts to fidget and move about, and focuses them to pay attention (print prioritizes mind over body). Only maintaining such a discipline can allow you to unravel the secrets held within books; secrets that might not reward you now but will prepare you for the future world of adulthood.

Schools, thus, focusing on delayed gratification, prioritized the future over the Now. They closed off the realm of immediate, worldly affairs to the young, even while opening up their minds to the world. In fact, Locke's eighteenth century metaphor of the child's mind being a *tabula rasa* (a blank tablet to be written on) closely follows from the world of print, believing that the child has to be prepared by the adult to become an adult.

Later in the same century, Rousseau in *Emile*, on the other hand, spoke of a child as a plant whose growth is organic and natural (Postman 1994, p. 60). Their "Now" is more important, he wrote, than an abstract adulthood. Their curiosity, spontaneity, and playfulness, he felt, should be nurtured, rather than be deadened, as it is by education. This is known as the romantic view. Freud and Dewey, both published books in 1899 (*The Interpretation of Dreams* and *The School and Society* respectively) that have posed a question that humankind has grappled with ever since. How to balance Locke and Rousseau? How to promote the claims of a child's instinctual nature against the claims of civilization?

In summary, we argue that print and subsequently schools were largely responsible for creating the gap between adults and youth.

But schools still rule 400 years later. So how come we are contending that though schools and institutions of learning continue to be strong pillars of society, youthhood might be disappearing? In fact, institutions that sequester young people from the "adult led real world," and prepare them within their four walls to enter this adult world have only multiplied in the form of higher education and vocational courses.

What *has changed* over the last two decades in India (and the world over) is the watershed we have reached in the field of communication technology. Electronic media (TV and Internet) rules today, and the reign of print is gradually beginning to decline. Our contention isn't that schools are going to disappear. We suggest that the nature of the classroom, and with it of youthhood, needs to transform drastically.

WHAT'S THE ROLE OF THE NEW SYMBOLIC ENVIRONMENT CREATED BY THE ELECTRONIC MEDIA IN NARROWING THE GENERATIONAL GAP THAT PRINT CREATED?

It's hardly a point of debate anymore that with the coming of electronic media, human life and our living experience have changed forever. We point to three major aspects of communication. For one, the speed of information has increased tremendously; second, information has become truly de-contextualized (it's not rooted in space or time); and lastly, the nature of the image as a poor keeper of secrets has been revealed. As a result of this, all kinds of non-local information are now accessible instantly to all ages of humans who don't need to be literate to understand it. At a time when our species is looking to control the world ever more, the age of electronic media (TV and the Internet) has made information become literally uncontrollable. Let's take Harold Innis' three effects of changes in communication technology which we used for studying print earlier and apply it to this new media to understand this paradox better.

1. The first effect, he said, was that new communication technology alters the things that are thought about. This is most palpable in the news industry that started with print but has grown exponentially with electronic media. "If it hasn't happened on TV, it hasn't happened at all," seems to be the new adage. The media circus (on TV and the Internet) that we all witnessed during the anticorruption movement in Delhi in August 2011 smothered out any other information (makes one think that if society could do without any other news for two weeks, do we really need it?) Whichever side you were on, all our thoughts were on the same place: the Ram Lila grounds (India's own Tahrir Square as some have dubbed it) where a brinkmanship game had us all guessing who would blink first—the government or Team Hazare.

   And unlike print, the information is instant with electronic media keeping us glued to the screens of our various devices relaying the latest breaking news from the Ram Lila grounds. We were given no space to think about anything else because the volume of this information was huge—24 * 7 * 100 (the number of news channels) * 14 (the number of days the drama lasted)—a figure we wouldn't want to waste our time counting except to say that it compares favorably to the numbers of people out in the streets, a statistic that was repeatedly touted as the single biggest achievement of the movement.

Of course, information in the electronic world is difficult to "manage"; it isn't sequential; in fact, it's this messiness, matching real life that makes the spectacle even more exciting like unscripted reality TV. Moreover, it's accessible to all with no control over the circumstances in which it is experienced, which means it's decontextualized (news from nowhere). Viewers in India, across all borders of class, age, sex, geography, caste, and religion, were moved by the image of a frail man on a fast to end corruption in the country and lo and behold, our symbolic minds had collectively been whipped into thinking of it as our age's own "second freedom movement," never mind that we are already a free country.

Need we say anything more about the power of the new communication technology to alter the things we are thinking about? Lest we sound cynical about this power, we'd like to state that the attention brought by the media and the "reality TV" format of the movement, to an issue lingering unsolved for decades, was invaluable. Another example that brings out how this power of whipping up an emotional frenzy can be beneficial for humanity happened earlier in the same year. In March 2011 when the electronic media connected the whole world to the misery that afflicted the Japanese due to the unprecedented tragic triple whammy, real resources and support flowed in to the devastated country thanks to this emotional outpouring midwifed by the electronic connect.

Beneficial or not, there is no denying the fact that electronic media has altered what we think of. We argue that a certain kind of crisis-mindedness has crept into our collective consciousness in the past couple of decades thanks to TV and Internet.

2. Next let's look at Innis' second effect: Communication technology changes what you think with. There is a deluge of images in the new media—pictures, cartoons, posters, advertisements, and film. Daniel Boorstein (as cited in Postman 1994, p. 72) has called this flood of images the "graphic revolution."

One would like to argue that the use of the Internet gained popularity when it became possible to transmit images over it (the role of pornography in making it an irresistible draw for many young men is well documented). While it was essentially a print medium, the Internet did not manage to catch the fancy of the young as it has in the last decade or so since bandwidth opened up for transmitting images and video. Especially with urban middle-class youth, the Internet is vying with TV for eyeballs and seemingly against all odds, it appears to be winning. And between print and Internet, there isn't even a contest anymore; the appeal of the former is clearly on the decline with the young.

In a study for 2010 done by the US Department of Labor's Bureau of Labor Statistics (http://www.bls.gov/news.release/rchives/atus_06222011.pdf), time spent reading for personal interest and playing games or using a computer/Internet for leisure varied greatly by age. Individuals aged 75 and above averaged 1.1 hours of reading per weekend day and 18 minutes playing games or using a computer/Internet for leisure. Conversely, individuals aged 15 to 19 *read for an average of 6 minutes per weekend day while spending 1.1 hours playing games or using a computer/Internet for leisure.* Remember this statistic is talking about computers and Internet usage for leisure and not for work, which too is increasing tremendously. In Indian metros as well, similar statistics would probably show up and analysts in the country too would agree that print is on the decline in comparison to visual electronic media.

Why is print losing its attraction for young people as compared to visual, electronic media? For answering this question, we need to remind ourselves that we are essentially a symbolic species. Language is nothing but a set of symbols the evolutionary niche humans have taken.

We re-present what is not present using symbols and images. We tell stories of our experiences in the past and those yet to come. We are essentially homo-narrans, the storytelling species. *With print the reader has to unlock an experience/story coded in abstract symbols connected by a difficult set of rules, while with graphics the experience is openly available and there for the readers' easy visual access.* In case of an image, there is minimal coding as compared to the cryptic nature of print.

Moreover, in print there is the opinion of the writer to contend with while in a picture, on the other hand, there are a lot more facts, or "hard news," and much less "editorializing." Unlike sentences, a picture represents what is out there pretty faithfully.

There are no rules of evidence, logic, or interpretation to which an image must conform. The viewer interprets what he/she wants, and it requires no skill, and different people could see the same picture differently. Is it any wonder that a writer concedes so readily that a picture is worth a thousand words? No contest.

Let us emphasize that though there is language involved, TV is essentially a visual medium (and so is the Internet with the high speed data bandwidths nowadays). We "watch" TV. The moving image is what draws us to it, not what we hear or read. But pictures also have a negative side. They call for an emotional response rather than the naturally intellectual one that print evokes. Rudolf Arnheim wrote in 1935 that because pictures evoke feelings and not reason, TV has the potential to put our minds to sleep (cited in Postman 1994, p. 73). His words ring true many years later. In a political contest, for example, the image of a candidate has become more important than his/her policies.

Returning to the example of the August 2011 movement against corruption in India, here too the hordes that thronged the site of the fast were moved by the "imagery" of a frail old man taking on the might of the state in a nonviolent Satyagraha harking back to Mahatama Gandhi. Not many who went to the Maidan in support of the modern-day Gandhi had read the Jan Lok Pal Bill whose smooth passage through the Parliament was their hero's main demand. Let there be no doubt, the entire movement was built on clever imagery and a series of symbolic visuals. It wouldn't be wrong, in fact, to call it a symbolic revolution, where Hazare's group sought to engage the heart rather than the mind of the people.

Yet, even with all its evils, the image marches on, capturing the imagination of the young like never before, ushering in an age where visual representation rules over experience. To capture a new place in a camera is much more important than experiencing it. More critical than the experience, is sharing the experience. That is, *the young seem more preoccupied with re-presenting rather than being present.* Tools like TV and Internet that allow us to invoke the past and the future with much greater ease than print have only hastened our journey away from the moment. Thus, the image revolution (spawned by the electronic media) has changed "what we think with" drastically.

3. The third effect, Innis claimed, which comes with new communication technology, is that the area in which thoughts are developed,

> changes. An oft-repeated phrase today, the world has become a "global village," owes its credence largely to electronic media. And it is the volume and reach of electronic media that has made the phrase, in turn, possibly the most repeated global cliché. But there is no doubt, that at least for a section of youth in every country, the entire world is their stage, and their ideas and thoughts concern more and more the abstracted arena of city, nation, and planet, rather than their immediate local neighborhood.

Thus, it is the very nature of the electronic medium which has drawn the young to it; indeed a huge wave of humanity has moved away from print, leaving it high and dry on the beaches of its past glory. For the first time in the history of mass communication, youth have got undifferentiated access to information, the same as adults.

This is not only because the image doesn't require symbolic literacy, as we argued earlier, but also because it is physically difficult to hide a TV or computer away on the top shelf of a cupboard, like you could a book. Another peculiarity of TV is that it operates round the clock. So it needs all-time fodder. For this, TV executives have to open up every possible closet and peek inside for possible content to air. Taboos tumble out with skeletons. Secrets only remain secrets until a desperately seeking TV executive exposes them. Typically, though there have been attempts to differentiate audiences, young people have obtained access to the most prurient of content with minimal of fuss.

As Neil Postman (1994, p. 82) says, "The bias and therefore the business of TV is to *move* information, not collect it." Thus, bastion after bastion of knowledge has been breached and by now it is a well-known fact that young people don't need to be in a classroom to access knowledge or a secret. It is available at their homes through TV and Internet, without the watchful chaperoning of any adult. The TV is the ultimate egalitarian medium of communication. *By eliminating the exclusivity of knowledge, TV and the Internet have, thus, closed the generation gap from the perspective of youth.*

Of course, there are many value-based cautions and alarms that should be raised against electronic media and indeed those have been shouted out from the idiot box by child development specialists and sociologists for at least two decades now. By providing indiscriminate access to adult secrets that include sex, violence, and incest, we are giving up the self-restraint that shame provided society, shame that was the creation of print thanks to the secrets it allowed adults to keep from the young.

Not only has this resulted in increased juvenile crime (as we mentioned earlier) but also brutalized the young at an early age without providing them with adequate psychological maturity to deal with the barrage. This could potentially lead to cynicism and despair among the young.

Unfortunately this is not the place to dwell into the ravages that electronic media wreaks upon the unformed mind. In fact, we want to stress here that the electronic media is only in its infancy; God alone knows what further psychological tsunamis are still to be unleashed by it upon humanity. What is becoming clear is that however amoral, as some feel, is electronic media's advent, we cannot wish it away. It's not only here to stay; in this Age of Expression, it is well on its way to becoming a new God.

The tectonic shifts in the knowledge monopolies that adults held over the last 400 years, we believe, will have a defining impact on the institution of school (and higher learning) as it exists today. Not only teachers, also parents, civil society, the entertainment industry, government policymakers, corporate managers, all need to take note of the impending shifts, if they are to keep themselves relevant in the coming times. Like the post office, many other institutions are poised to be buried under the flow of the times and if the school wants to escape that fate, society needs to transform the concept of the classroom very quickly and make it more in rhythm to the new communication technology that is taking over from print.

CHAPTER HIGHLIGHTS

We believe it's time parents, teachers, policymakers, media people, and civil society stopped clinging to an archaic concept of the classroom. The take-over of the young mind by the electronic media is already having a profound impact on the classroom and, indeed, on the idea of youthhood itself. As the gap between adults and youth narrows in terms of knowledge (albeit not in experience), young people should be encouraged to act more and more in the real world and learn from it. Yet adults never seem to learn. The gap is gone, but the concept of the gap that remains in the heads of adults still defines policymaking for the young. The illusion of being in charge continues to blind adults the world over.

In the next chapter, we argue that in India, since Independence, adults have tried to cling on to the hierarchies and status quo between the young and them. Till now they have succeeded but if they don't wake up, their world-view is in mortal danger of being overrun by the psychological tsunamis already unleashed by the electronic media and many more still to come. If they want the Ram Lila Maidan and the anticorruption movement to be a mere footnote to history, then adults will have to change the attitude that print has given them for the past 400 years. The arrogance that came from superior knowledge is as much of an anachronism in this electronic age as is the post office.

Given the leveled and democratized "knowledge scape" brought about by the electronic media, adults should stop focusing their interaction with youth on "teaching" them how to become better adults. The young will figure it out on their own. Instead of trying to prepare youth for the future, adults, we believe, need to give serious consideration towards creating spaces where youth can learn from experiences and live the moment to its fullest.

2

If You Approach the Ocean with a Spoon, Won't It Look Like a Drop?

In this chapter we move out of the classroom and into the streets—from the symbolic world to the real one. We study the participation of youth in political and developmental processes. Here, too, like the classroom, we argue that the concept of youthhood and how to nurture young people's energy drop by drop for the common good needs a massive makeover. "You must contribute to society. Give back something. Even if it's just a drop in the ocean." This is what parents, teachers, and politicians have always told the young. This well-meaning inspiration has been a part of our nation's discourse with its young for decades. And the youth, right from the Independence movement up to the first anticorruption movement of the seventies and now the second one, have tried to heed their elders' advice.

But the truth is that in spite of the efforts at replenishing the ocean, it only looks further depleted. Corruption, communalism, and casteism continue to pollute the minds of our political leadership. Despite the India growth story (or some say because of it), the country's statistics on development, justice, and value-based leadership are damning. Numbers do not necessarily translate into growth, and growth should not be confused with development. Economic reforms may have accelerated growth, but they have also exacerbated inequalities and eroded social welfare provided by the State. While on the one hand, we are now the third largest economy in terms of purchasing power parity, with consistent growth rates of 6–9 percent in the last five years, on the other hand the levels of poverty and inequality have grown hugely. Every third poor person in the world is an Indian; every third illiterate in the world is an Indian too and more than half of the children under five in India are malnourished (Oxfam India 2010). Some estimates put the "real" unemployment (though there are jobs, people do not have the right skills) as high as 12–15 percent. As a result, real (and virtual) revolutions rage round the republic and the Constitution is under daily threat.

At the same time, per capita income has never been so high. India boasts of as many as 25 among the 100 richest people on the planet. Have we abandoned the common spaces, the ocean, and got busy tending to personal islands? Have we forgotten that our island is connected at the hip to the ocean? That they are part of one and the same continuum? When you try to pick out something from its universe, the universe comes with it. Can you pick up one end of a stick and hope the other stays on the ground? Modern man seems to believe he can. This delusion has led to the greatest paradox that humanity faces today: *we are so self-absorbed, yet so suicidal.* You must have heard this story about Mullah Naseeruddin, the wise fool of Turkey (see Figure 2.1). The Mullah is found chuckling by his friend on the street one morning. "Why are you laughing, Mullah Naseeruddin?" the friend asks.

"You know, that Amir ... I am going to teach him a lesson," Mullah replies with a big grin on his face.

"How is that?"

"You see, he slaps me hard on the chest every time he meets me, and it hurts! I have told him not to, but he does not listen. So today I have tied a stick of dynamite on my chest under my coat ... hee hee hee. Now we will see who gets hurt when he slaps me!"

Figure 2.1: We Are So Self-absorbed, Yet So Suicidal

Source: Authors.

Of course, the young alone are not responsible for our suicidal tendencies that are showing up in the ravages to the ocean. But because they stand to be most hurt by the rampant neglect of the common spaces, they are the ones, some feel, whose duty it is to contribute their drops to the ocean. In the recent past, we too at Pravah have appealed to the young to do their duty, to help heal the world, to volunteer for the right causes. Our programs, until recently, have largely focused young people on taking up action projects to create social change. Yet, as we said before, the state of the ocean has only deteriorated (in terms of human development parameters) since we started our crusade.

Of course, our alumni have made significant impact and are continuing to do so. But we recognize that in a country of 1.2 billion people, the numbers they impact can never be enough. For the scale of change needed, we in turn need a massive cadre of youth interested in taking ownership of common spaces in a sustainable long-term way. The problem has been that when we appeal to young people to join us in creating long-term systemic change (as against mere participation in protests and rallies), we get, typically, only a handful of takers who respond enthusiastically.

Is it because our appeal is like water off a duck's back for the larger mainstream of urban youth for whom careers are of paramount importance today when there are so many opportunities of economic advancement in India? Can't mainstream youth have social change in their radars, except when it affects their career opportunities directly like the highly emotive subjects of corruption and job reservation? Or are they merely content with putting their drops into the ocean through protest, win–lose, and us-versus-them initiatives? Is it too ambitious for us to hope that young people will learn to use processes of systemic and long-term impact that actually help them understand the connection between Self and Society? Will they ever end up taking full ownership of common spaces rather than the token efforts we see today? Set against such a formidable barrier, is our mobilization pitch—"Let's change the world"—somewhat over the top? Can today's youth really change the world drop by drop?

We know it's not common to start a story with a (qualified) admission of failure in these days of shameless self-promotion. But it is from this admission that we have gained our greatest insights into youth development so far. After much soul searching and reams of research we found that our problem lies in a mistaken point of view, that youth can be galvanized toward their future. That they should view their contribution as a drop that will replenish the ocean slowly, and that the ocean will sparkle again by the time they gain adulthood. That's where we have found the nub of the problem.

Young people, in reality, are not so interested in a distant and virtual future. Much like the rest of humanity, they are interested in a vibrant *now*.

Thus, to mobilize this group in huge numbers, we need to recognize that *every drop is in itself an ocean*. Their inner ocean needs as much attention as the outer world. We need to remember that a young person's journey starts with the Self; that youthhood is first and foremost a time for making first impressions; of seeking and forming an identity. Only when a young person's personal needs, intentions, desires, hopes, and fears are organically connected to the common spaces can we expect social change to become a sustainable quest. Youth need to internalize that Society and the Self are more than just linked at the hip—they are one and the same. Jan, Man, One. This is the new anthem we have begun to sing at Pravah, and it is giving us spectacular results in mobilizing and inspiring young people. Our mobilization appeal to the young (and as a consequence our programming too) has changed to: "Come let the world change you today," as against: "Do your bit to change the world because you will reap later what you sow now." By foregrounding the Self, we plug into their identity quest which in turn can only be accomplished by acting in the real world.

We talk more about our experiences in the field of youth-centric development (as against youth *for* development) in the next chapter. This kind of work with the youth, we strongly believe, in turn, has a pivotal bearing on how vibrant common spaces in a society are. We feel that to engage large numbers of mainstream youth to tend these spaces we have to help them understand how the ocean outside is connected to the ocean that flows inside them.

Two years ago, when we were getting mixed results in mobilizing youth for social change, we asked ourselves this question: when, in this country's history, has a young person's own present been organically linked to a social common good? We undertook primary and secondary research ranging from the early forties to the first decade of this century to try and understand the different lenses that society wore across different points of time (see Annexure 1 for the contours of this study). This research became the mainstay of this book. In the next section, we give you a glimpse of our findings as we zoom into a point of time in our history when our political discourse was abuzz with the voices of the young. Youth were engaged en masse in long-term systemic social and political change. And here we are talking of decades' long systemic involvement, not fortnight revolutions. We are referring to the years leading up to the country's freedom and the time just after we became an independent republic. Large numbers of youth joined the movement and electoral politics thereafter. But somewhere along the way the tide turned and the numbers involved in nation-building have dwindled drastically.

HOW AND WHEN DID WE DROWN OUT THE VOICE OF YOUNG PEOPLE?

Amongst the clamor of the demographic dividend imminent in 2020, when we take over the crown of being the youngest nation in the world, amongst the babble of parents, narrators, interpreters, journalists, corporate managers, politicians, and bureaucrats, about what we should be doing to reap that dividend, amidst all the media frenzy about corruption and terrorism, and amidst the loud laments of righteous civil society organizations about the lack of quality politicians, are we even listening to the voices of the young? Or have they got drowned in the flow of a narrative marching on toward its second "tryst with destiny?"

There is no doubt about our status as a lumbering giant poised to make our mark on the world, but we have been there before. We are talking of 1947 when we became free and a just, equitable, and prosperous future beckoned. But we missed that chance as is evident from our dismal records on social, environmental, economic, and human rights parameters.

Even so, our luck seems to have turned again. The broad sweep of history, the flow of circumstances, a functioning democracy, some astute economic decisions, and a giant domestic market have washed us ashore on a promising looking "treasure island." If we exploit it well, many claim it will restore us to the status of *sone ki chidiya*,[1] a preeminent global position. But history seldom gives third chances, and if we don't make good this time, 2020 could well turn into a demographic disaster.

For a positive denouement this time round, we believe we have to learn from the mistakes that we made during the first decade of the founding of our republic. Promise in the air, trust on every sleeve, freedom gained after such a long struggle, an independent republic enshrined in a great constitution, a brand new ship on a voyage to distant shores, how did we lose our way? When did things start to go wrong?

[1]This is a metaphor used to denote the wealth and riches in ancient India; the goose that lays the golden egg.

Why were we unable to make good the promises outlined in the Constitution of India?

The answer to these questions, we believe, holds the key to the renewal of our society. We have focused in this chapter on participation of youth in politics as an indicator of the roles played by the young in society. No doubt, youth participation in other spheres, like family, careers, religion, etc., are also an important part of the discourse, and we turn our attention to these areas subsequently in the next chapters. However, we decided to start with political representation and governance indicators because we believe they have a significant impact on all other roles that young people play in society and because most commentators declare that what the country needs most today is value-based political leadership, especially among the youth.

It was very different in the thirties and forties. Our research shows that India's freedom was obtained by, amongst others, a large cohort of young people. Thousands took on leadership roles based on the principles of patriotism and sacrificed their careers and lives for the common good. Of course, they rode on the guidance of adults in their own generation and the groundswell created by actions of youth in preceding ones.

When Jawaharlal Nehru was chosen to head the Congress Party at the age of 40, in Lahore in 1929, Gandhi said: "The appointment of Jawaharlal Nehru as the captain is the proof of the trust the nation reposes in its youth. Jawaharlal Nehru alone can do little. The youth of this country must be his arms and eyes. Let them prove worthy of the trust." And they did. Youth participation and leadership during the Indian freedom movement is well documented (Altbach 1970).

The age profile of the first and second Lok Sabha emphasizes this fact very well. In the first Lok Sabha, as many as 26 percent of the MPs were between 25 and 40 years of age while in the second Lok Sabha it went up even higher, up to 32 percent (Mathew 2009)!

Largely it was the freedom fighters (the poster boys and girls as well as the thousands of lesser known ones) who jumped into the electoral fray at the dawn of a new India, hoping to contribute to the nation-building task as significantly as they had to ousting the empire. Like an ocean on the march, young students, farmers, lawyers, and workers, flowing side by side with their elder guides after sweeping aside the bulwarks of an Empire, presented themselves on the deck of the brand new ship, ready to chart its next voyage. Commentators of the times are unanimous in their view that the contribution of youth in those heady days was no drop in the ocean; they constituted the ocean itself, especially during the final days of the freedom struggle.

That endgame of the movement drew young people in like never before in a myriad of ways ranging from responsible citizenship to wresting justice, from simply boycotting British cotton and wearing homespun khadi to bombing government offices. Not only were they participating in large numbers, young people were leading the movement from the front. Bhagat Singh, Chandrashekhar Azad, and thousands of others were below 40 years of age at the peak of their efforts toward gaining freedom for their country. It was an upswell of youth citizenship action—both constructive and destructive—like this country had never seen before and has not experienced since (except, arguably, during the socialist uprisings led by Jaiprakash Narayan and Ram Manohar Lohiya in the seventies and the start of the Naxalite movement in the same decade). After Independence too, as evinced in the number of young parliamentarians in the first two Lok Sabhas, youth led from the front.

Alas, youth participation in politics and governance has declined steadily since then; the ocean has been dwindling to a drop. In the current Lok Sabha, 2009, the percentage of members of Parliament (MPs) within the age bracket 25 to 40 years has reduced drastically to a paltry 6.3 percent (from a high of 32 percent in the second Lok Sabha). Also startling is the drop in the number of MPs in the next age category (41 to 55 years) between the first and the latest Lok Sabha: down from 54 percent to 33.5 percent. On the other hand, the number of elders (56 years and above) in the Lok Sabha has seen a spectacular jump in the same period, from 0.2 percent to 11. 7 percent; a staggering 1,200 percent (see Table 2.1 and Figure 2.2).

How did this happen? When did the tide turn? How did the ocean of youth dwindle to a drop? People who work with the young in this country

Table 2.1: Age-wise Representation in the Lok Sabha

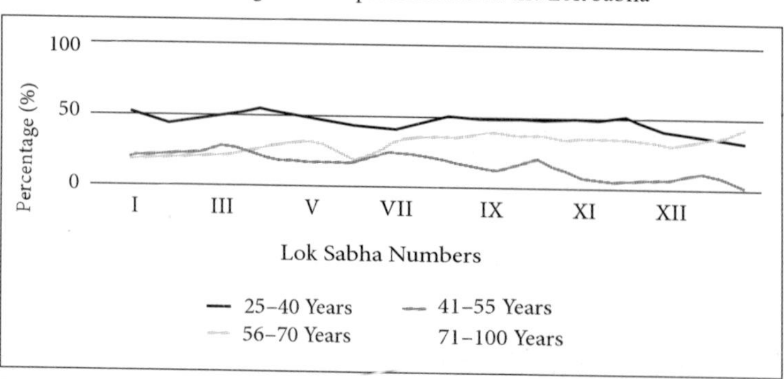

Source: Mathew 2009.

Figure 2.2: Who Is Championing Youth Causes?

Source: Authors.

(policymakers, corporate and media mandarins, educators, NGOs, etc.) can learn many lessons from studying one of the most significant turning points in our history.

We believe something changed in the way the elders of the freedom movement were viewing youth in those days just after Independence. While putting together the founding principles, they debated on the responsibilities and duties of each segment of society. Sometime then, acting on a reductionist and exclusivist point of view, the "elders" decided to approach the ocean of youth with a spoon. And if you expect a drop then that's what you get. The adults decided to shoulder a large part of the governance load onto themselves and asked the youth to go back into the classrooms in preparation for their adulthood. Their turn would come, the young were told. They were urged to reduce their roles back to their studies, careers, and families. This was noted by Altbach who comments: "Following Indian independence, the relationship between the student body of activists and the governing Indian National Congress became strained when the Congress encouraged students to leave politics to the adult members of the movement" (Altbach 1970). Twenty years earlier, Gandhi had urged young people to join the movement, only to change his mind in 1947, when he stated that students must "eschew active politics ... [because] a student's duty is to study various problems that require solution. His time for action comes after he finishes his studies" (Gandhi 1947).

Approaching the young thus with a spoon, the country's leaders circumscribed the young person's role in tending to common spaces; but while they were not encouraged to own these spaces, they were urged not to forget about them altogether either. They were still duty bound to "put your drop into the ocean."

And yet, the youth energy would not be quelled. Earlier, we noted that a sizeable percentage of MPs in the first and second Lok Sabha were 25 to 40 years old. It is true, young people did join politics in large numbers as a career post Independence. But it is when we juxtapose this information with another piece of data that our real point begins to emerge. No doubt the first two Lok Sabhas had a large percentage of parliamentarians but the Parliament is a legislative body and not necessarily the governing body. It is the cabinet that governs, ensuring that constitutional acts/laws get translated into strategies and plans. Cabinet members are also responsible for implementation of the targets by the executive.

When we studied the average age of the first Cabinet (that is, only ministers with cabinet rank) we were somewhat shocked by our finding. *The mean age of the first Cabinet was as high as 54 years* (only one— Jagjivan Ram—was in age bracket of 25–40 years, and even he was just months short of 40 on August 15, 1947). Needless to say, the average age of the cabinet has been increasing ever since. *In the latest Lok Sabha of 2009, it stands at 62.7 years with not even a single minister of cabinet rank below 40.*

What were the "elders of the nation" thinking when they were putting together the first cabinet? How do you justify an average age of 54 years for this apex body with one token minister below the age of 40 when 26 percent of the representatives were from the age group of 25–40 years? It were as if the elders, while thanking the youth effusively after Independence for lending their energy to a great cause, were telling them in the same breath: "Now that the cause is won, would you please get out of the way and let us elders govern."

By 2020 we'll be the youngest nation in the world, ruled by one of the oldest cabinets in the world (Pravah 2009).

In the G20 group of world leaders two years ago, our Prime Minister at 78 looked starkly out of place rubbing shoulders with Obama at 49, David Cameron at 44, Angela Merkel at 49, Hu Jintao at 62, Sarkozy at 55, Laila Roussa at 64, Medvedev at 44. No wonder, Obama calls him "the wise old man" (see Figure 2.3).

Figure 2.3: G20 Meet

Source: Authors.

We have the dubious honor of the oldest head of state in the world but also the highest average age of the cabinet (see Table 2.2).

Table 2.2: Youngest Nation, Oldest Cabinet

Country	Head of state	Age	Average age of cabinet	Median age of population[2]
India	Manmohan Singh	78	64	26
Italy	Silvio Berlusconi	74	54	44
China	Hu Jintao	68	61	35
Brazil	Roussa	64	60	29
Japan	Naoto Kan	64	59	45
Indonesia	Susilo B. Yudhoyono	61	56	28
France	Nicolas Sarkozy	55	56	40
Canada	Stephen Harper	51	53	41
USA	Barack Obama	49	58	37
Russia	Dmitri Medvedev	44	52	39
UK	David Cameron	43	50	40

Source: Thakur 2010.

[2]This is the age that divides a population into two numerically equal groups—that is, half the people are younger than this age and half are older.

The current average age of the Indian cabinet at 64 years is almost two and half times the country's median age of 26. Most other countries boast a difference of a decade or so between the cabinet's average age and the population's median age. As a corollary to the decision to keep young people out of governance, we argue that youth *ownership for common spaces* plummeted (corroborated among other indicators by the massive decline in young parliamentarians) over the years, giving way first to apathy and then to cynicism in today's post-ideological age. Participation in political processes, nurtured as a right during the freedom movement, has slowly turned into a duty. A duty ... as in someone telling you what to do, rather than it coming from within. As in a boring chore, rather than an opportunity to transform your life. When a dynamic like this enters the social organism, it slowly starts to decay from within.

Our experience in mobilizing young people during the nineties echoes these trends. We found that young people have been increasingly focused on competitive exams and their careers and have found little time for social engagement. Except for a brief upsurge in the seventies and eighties, youth leadership and ownership for common spaces have been on the decline. The nineties and most of the first decade of this century could be termed the neoliberal decades when the juggernaut of the market, combined with the indifferent attention to youth affairs by the government, brought careers to the center stage for youth, to the near exclusion of other spaces. Efforts, time, and energy of youth and their support groups have been largely directed toward employability, entrepreneurship, or work performance. The recent anticorruption movement is the blip that might signify the changing times and the new symbolic environment ushered in by the electronic media that we talked about in the previous chapter. But it's too early to tell whether this will bring about sustained participation in political processes. Will the youth of this neoliberal decade have the stomach for the long haul that is required to change things structurally in a working, argumentative, diverse, caste-based representative democracy?

As we said before, in this chapter we have focused only on youth participation in political processes to bring out the radical change in how society viewed youth before and after Independence. Other spaces like family, careers, education, and religion have also undergone massive alterations in this period. We devote a chapter later to a more holistic view of changing the youthscape.

Before we move on from politics and governance, we would like to note another marker that illustrates the neglect of youth issues by the political leadership, namely, the treatment meted out to youth affairs by the concerned ministry. In fact, ever since Independence, youth affairs has not even been deemed worthy of a separate ministry (and, thus, in a sense the nation's mindshare). When it was finally separated from the Human Resource Development (HRD) ministry (and set up as a separate ministry in May 2000) and given charge to a full cabinet minister, the government, in its wisdom, decided to bundle it together with sports. It was only in April 2008 that two separate departments were set up under the Ministry of Youth Affairs and Sports with separate secretaries—for Youth Affairs and Sports.

By appointing a 73-year-old as cabinet minister for Youth Affairs and Sports in United Progressive Alliance (UPA) 2, the message given out by the Prime Minister was amply clear for even those whose ears aren't cocked to such frequencies (see Figure 2.4). The recent appointment of Jitendra Singh, 41, is a welcome redressal of a long-pending demand. We hope he is able to live up to the expectations that naturally follow a long drought. Of course, just being 41 does not necessarily mean he will be able to fulfill the aspirations of the young. It is not age alone that defines someone as young. After all, Abdul Kalam, Sheela Dixit, and Anna Hazare all became youth icons after they turned 70.

Figure 2.4: Ex Minister of Youth Affairs Proving His Credentials

Source: Authors.

SO HOW DO WE DEFINE YOUTH? SIMPLY BY AGE?

We have been harping on about age as if it were the only defining typology in the discourse of what it means to be a young person. This is as good a place as any in our narrative for admitting that we are doing a disservice to the former Minister for Youth Affairs by being a little dismissive of his credentials for looking after the concerns of young people merely because he was almost five times the chronological age of the lower range of how his ministry categorizes youth (15 to 35 years). After all, who doesn't retain some of the traits of youth well into their advancing years? Don't all men claim to be little boys at heart?

All the same, age has been used as a marker for many policy decisions concerning youth. Permissions for voting, driving, liquor/cigarettes, adult movies, and marriage are all legislated by age. The age definition is widely debated though; the United Nations and most of the "North" countries categorize youth in the age group 15 to 24 years (and now with advancing puberty from 12 to 24) while many in the "South," citing late opportunities and delayed independence from the family in the developing world as the reasons, have pushed that limit up to 35 years.

Apart from age, what are the typologies that define the category of youth? There is some level of consensus among theorists, on the other nonchronological *traditions of the sociology of youth*. These traditions are characterized by Wyn and White (Jeffs and Smith 1999, pp. 45–66) as *(a)* youth transitions, *(b)* youth development, and *(c)* youth subcultures. To this we'd like to add *(d)* Karl Mannheim's generational/context theory (Mannheim 1952). A quick study of all these traditions is essential because from each of them emerge relevant attributes that could form the *inputs for a lot of the recommendations* in this book (see Box 2.1).

Box 2.1: Youth Theories and Significant Takeaways for the Youth Sector

1. Youth transitions: Youthhood is seen as a time of transition to adulthood, from dependence to independence. Youth programs need to develop appropriate skills, such as leadership, decision-making, problem solving, and conflict resolution, to facilitate this transition.
2. Development stages of youth: Youthhood is a specific cognitive, psychological, and physical period of growth. It is a time when the mind is getting wired and forming impressions of the world. These

first impressions can be defining, and if learning strategies could be developed to provide greater opportunities for forming impressions and processing these along with the young person, it may be of immense importance in a world where knowledge is getting democratized but where adults gate-keep the access to experiences.

3. Youth subcultures and life style choices: Young people express their rejection of dominant culture by creating subcultures based on choices of music, fashion, language, sports, etc. Youth development strategies will need to include modernity, consumption experiences, and connection into global subcultures.

Source: Compiled by the authors.

The first of these traditions looks at the way in which youthhood is constructed and structured through the institutions that "process" the *transitions to adulthood.* We have already spoken of it as originating from Locke in Chapter 1. These transitions include leaving the parental home and establishing new living arrangements, completing full-time education, forming close and stable relationships outside the family often resulting in marriage and children, getting a job of sorts, etc. This theory is largely built around the concept of young people striving to gain independence and hence becoming adults.

The problem with this theory is that we have to imagine a mainstream in which the majority of young people neatly go forward in a unidirectional way toward some magical moment when adulthood is conferred. In a diverse country like India, where young people across geographies, gender, and class differ hugely in opportunities and thus the timing (even viability in some cases) of attainment of "adulthood" markers mentioned above, the theory runs into obvious difficulties. Further, there seems a glorification of an economistic view, which, particularly for young men, sees full-time employment as the pivotal signifier of adulthood (see Jeffs and Smith 1999). For young women, marriage and motherhood tend to be pivotal signifiers of adulthood, even if they are earning members of their families. This patriarchal view sees women's role as nurturers of the future workforce and is also informed by an economistic lens. However, this theory does have some takeaways that are relevant for youth facilitators. *Strategies for development of life skills (leadership, problem solving, conflict resolution, decision-making, and such)* have no doubt originated from the needs of youth outlined by the transition theory. We will delve deeper into this in a later section.

We run into similar problems with the *second tradition of defining youth.* This classification rests on the *developmental stages of youth.* Young people are seen as making systematic progression in a certain order through a series of phases of cognitive, psychological, and physical developments (Jeffs and Smith 1999). Except, when you begin to consider individual biographies, they differ considerably and there isn't one universal path, nor is there some fixed end point. Not all young people are rebellious, not all are energetic, and certainly many not so eager to learn; in fact many "adults" could claim to be "better" at all of the above than many "youth." Apart from differences of age, there are also differences of gender, caste, and class that cannot be ignored. While young men are socialized to be ambitious and nurture a killer instinct, young women are expected to nurture the mothering instinct and become homemakers. All the same, this tradition is also useful because it supplies us with one nugget that is universal: *youthhood is a time of psychological first impressions.* Young people begin to engage extensively with society for the first time and its impact on them in these "first" interactions is huge. Their minds start to get wired about the outer world in a more defined way. While we definitely do not subscribe to the view that young people are putty in the hands of society and can be molded, we do believe that denying the universality of the "impressionable" nature of youth might be a folly in political correctness. Here too, *learning strategies tailored to this possibility* of society impacting young people, even as young people experiment with changing the world, have served us well.

The third definition, lifestyle choice and youth subculture,[3] is not as relevant to the Indian scenario, though youth communities following certain subcultures around fashion, sports, music, and films do exist in India. Virtual communities too, are making their presence felt increasingly among the young. But, as research has shown, these subcultures in India are hugely porous and flexible unlike the "gangs" and music "scenes" of the USA and UK. While acknowledging this, we would be myopic if we were to dismiss the considerable and increasing impact on the young of the lifestyle choices they make, driven by consumerism among urban middle-class youth in particular. *Modernity, consumption experiences,*

[3]Youth subcultures are a form of subversive resistance or counterculture to the dominant social norms that are normally expressed through fashion, style, music, etc. The hippies, punks, rockers, and greasers are commonly known youth subcultures in the West. According to Kaustav Sengupta, we do not have indigenous subcultures in India (see ingene.blogsport.com).

and connection into global subcultures are yearnings essential to include in our future strategies of youth development (Lukose 2005).

Finally the last classification is Karl Mannheim's contextual/generational influences on youth, though it cannot strictly be called a theory. Even so, his observations in the early twenties of the last century were prophetic in many ways: Youth have "a common location in the social and historical process, [which] thereby limit[s] them to a specific range of experiences, predisposing them for a certain characteristic mode of thought and experience, and a characteristic type of historically relevant action" (as quoted in Jeffs and Smith 1999). His main idea is that the context that young people grow up in, necessarily defines how they behave. Every generation has its icons and its defining moments that separate them from their predecessors creating trends and fashions that could be termed as mass youth culture.

It's true that cataclysmic events like the Independence movement or World War II can change the way those who witness them view the world, but the problem with this theory is that this it is not merely a youth phenomenon. The entire thinking population, not only the young, gets affected by events in their immediate environment and begins to behave in a certain way. This criticism has been countered by Mannheim's followers who contend that it is young people who get affected the most by such events due to their psychosocial makeup and, therefore, it is they who might react outwardly to such events more than "adults." They claim that it is *young people who are the most impressionable as actors and spectators when they collide with or ride on such contexts.* This theory has a very important bearing on the youth scene today. The safe, stable looking context of the Cold War days has suddenly sprung a million air leaks. The emerging vacuum in viable political and systemic ideologies has led to the concomitant crisis of Climate Change and global terrorism and systemic corruption that are streamed into our houses by scores of 24 × 7 news channels and social media sites. It's being made out to be an age of multiple crises; "poised at the brink of cataclysmic changes" is the abiding story beamed at us by the electronic media. What is true is not important—the impression from the images is of impending chaos.

And young people are taking notice. Again. As against the earlier cynical career-oriented nineties and the early years of this century, a palpable change in youth attitudes seems to be emerging in the past few years. The anticorruption movement in India and the mutinies in the Arab world are a case in point. We dwell on this trend in considerable detail later but suffice it to say here that practitioners on the ground are reporting that the drop of Active Citizenship is beginning to grow into a trickle and hopefully this could turn into a river, a river that can pour into and reenergize the ocean of youth participation in politics and governance again. Thus, in a sense, the context and how state and nonstate actors create the right kind of spaces within this context for youth citizenship, could become the catalyst for reviving the spirit of the Independence movement among young people. A lot still needs to be done to achieve this though. Recommendations in this book attempt to outline possible responses for riding this contextual dividend, and as we argue, also boost our capacity to reap the demographic one in 2020.

One qualifier is critical before we end this chapter. The mind-boggling diversity of the age group defined as youth in India, blurs the already confusing picture further. Youth may be 40 percent of the population (almost 500 million people), but this is by no means a homogeneous group. The rural elite and marginalized, the urban rich and poor, and the rigid complex borders of caste, gender, and religion, all create different needs, aspirations, hopes and fears among youth and thus require separate strategies. Any youth program or policy needs to take into account the differences that exist between young people, based on their sex, region, caste, and class.[4] There are also migrant youth, young people living in disturbed areas, such as the North East and Kashmir, and young people with special needs. Each of these groups has its own peculiarities and realities and though they may all fit into the category of youth from a chronological perspective, the diversity is great and needs to be recognized which is why country-wide programs need to be decentralized and community-led to be effective.

We try to make sense of the big picture of youth engagement in India in the next chapter, even as we try to paint in the swathes of diversity of Indian youth into the same canvas. Though our bias and major experience may be toward urban middle-class youth, we will be addressing Indian youth as a whole unless stated otherwise.

[4]A percentage of 51.6 Indian youth are male while 48.4 percent are female. A percentage of 69.3 come from rural areas; 30.7 percent live in urban areas; 15.7 percent belong to Scheduled Castes and 7.8 percent to Scheduled Tribes. A percentage of 80.6 are Hindus, while 13.2 percent are Muslims, in addition to Christians, Sikhs, and others. A percentage of 71 are literate and 53.8 percent work. (See Census of India 2001, Office of Registrar General, Government of India, New Delhi.)

CHAPTER HIGHLIGHTS

To sum up, in this chapter we have argued that critical to obtaining a just, equitable, and value-based society is the way policymakers have viewed youth since India gained its Independence. While young people played a significant role in helping secure our freedom, youth participation in politics and governance has steadily declined since then, and this is only one of the indicators of the declining ownership of young people for common spaces. Apart from a brief resurgence in the sixties and seventies, when young people rooted for systemic and long-term change, there has not been a great level of youth involvement in social affairs of nation-building. We believe we are on the brink of another significant opportunity to draw young people into cocreating common spaces. We believe that this picture may be changing, owing in the main to the watershed in the symbolic environment brought on by the electronic media. As we looked at the various traditions of the sociology of youth, there are some significant takeaways for those of us wishing to work with this group. First comes from the theory that looks at youth as a stage of transition to adulthood, and this has implications on how we engage with young people so as to develop appropriate leadership and life skills to smoothen this transition. In the context of defining youth on the basis of developmental stages of young people, what is of relevance to us is that youth is the time of first impressions and, therefore, learning strategies that can be tailored to take advantage of this will have a huge impact on young people. If we define youth vis-à-vis lifestyle choice and subculture, then modernity, consumption experiences, and connection into global subcultures will need to be included in our future strategies of youth development. Finally, as we look at contextual/generational influences on youth, we believe that a conducive environment/context can pull in young people to participate actively in civil society.

In the next chapter, we study the big picture of the youth scene in the country and the different elements within it. We also explore how different stakeholders have responded to the needs of young people.

3

What Are the Different Lenses for Viewing Youth?

As we noted in the previous chapter, young people showed up at the ship of a newly independent India for crew duty but were asked to become passengers instead by the elders. They were told to go back to their studies and careers and leave the governance of the country to the more experienced leaders. The navigators of independent India, thus, denied young people the right to be a part of giving direction to the nation. Today these powerful and experienced navigators take all the policy decisions for the rest of the citizens, including the youth. The navigators themselves are divided in the way they would like to shape the future of youth in our country because they wear different lenses. To make matters worse, many believe that the current problems of social justice and human development arise because the young have become increasingly self-centered, not willing to commit even their tiny drop to the ocean. Others claim, there are young people who engage with the world but their actions are misled and their energy destructively channelized; the enduring image of young people stoning buses, torching cars, and rioting on the streets are cited to substantiate this point of view. By depicting sensational acts of youth indulging in vandalism far more extensively than the instances of youth nurturing common spaces, the media has played a significant role in shaping public perceptions of youth.

Another lens, newly developed over the last decade, is the economistic lens increasingly worn by government and corporate mandarins. Their take on youth is far more positive. In the changed economic scenario, youth are being exhorted to become part of another independence movement; a movement that will free them from the shackles of poverty by giving purchasing power into their hands and in the bargain turning India into a global superpower. This lens views youth as a huge market of consumers as well as the future workforce that will fuel double digit growth.

The statistics back this economistic view of youth. India is witnessing a demographic transition. It is home to one of the largest and fastest-growing youth populations in the world. Currently it has 330 million people aged at 10–24 and if one goes by the national definition of youth (ages 13–35), then youth constitute 40 percent of the population (UN Economic and Social Commission for Asia and the Pacific 2007). This huge cohort is difficult to ignore. Its values, attitudes, and skills will shape the country's future.

By 2020, India is slated to become the youngest nation (average age 29 years as compared to China's 37, Japan's 48, and Europe's 49) (Basu 2007; Upadhyay 2010). Its dependency ratio will drop from 0.6 to 0.4. This means that the number of people who work against those who don't will increase substantially. If this increased cadre of youth were productively employed, it's true that our gross domestic product (GDP) could see an unprecedented jump, as has been seen before in the case of Canada and Ireland. This is called the demographic dividend.

Thus, youth are being painted into the nation's big picture in a myriad different ways. It all depends on the lens worn by the navigator (see Figure 3.1). As of now, the navigators (stakeholders) have used four broad ways of viewing young people: *(a)* youth as consumers and the future workforce, *(b)* youth as clients of development programs, *(c)* youth as instruments of social change, and *(d)* youthhood as a unique stage in life for learning about the world and themselves. We will analyze how these strategies are reflected in the different institutional responses to youth, keeping in mind that organizations sometimes adopt overlapping strategies.

Figure 3.1: How Clear Are Our Views of Youth?

Source: Authors.

IS EMPLOYMENT THE MAGIC BULLET?

When policymakers view young people *through an economistic lens*, they tend to reduce them to the roles of workers who need to be trained in marketable skills so that they can contribute to economic growth and national prosperity. There is also the role of consumer thrust upon young people when viewing them from an economistic lens, but more on that later. For an economistic policymaker, education becomes tantamount to training inputs that ensure a student's successful entry into the market. As per the latest education policies, following earlier neoliberal trends, the main purpose of education seems to be to develop high quality human resources that will help to fuel double-digit growth for the nation.[1]

Vocational training, as against a liberal arts education, is being seen as the mantra for empowering youth and taking advantage of the demographic dividend. The objective of the recently established National Skills Development Commission is to skill/upskill 150 million people in India including persons from rural areas by the year 2022, mainly by fostering private sector initiatives in skill development programs (Ministry of Labour and Employment 2010). This aims to harness the energy of young people presumably to reap the demographic dividend. The private sector has taken up the challenge with unprecedented gusto. Every industrial association is drawing up skills and competency maps and pumping money into developing these abilities in young people: Confederation of Indian Industry (CII), National Association of Software and Services Companies (NASSCOM), vocational training NGOs, and other entrepreneurs have all set up employment and employability initiatives. In fact, private and government venture funds have invested in a big way to provide for the skilling movement. Yes, one cannot but call it a movement because the nationalistic overtones are obvious.

Optimistic though this view might be, it is too economistic in its main line of argument. It reduces the young to the role of productive workers or generous spenders (unlike their thrifty parents). The media has been co-opted by the corporate sector to promote consumption as a significant life experience.

The argument of the mandarins goes on to claim that youth should therefore be engaged in careers or in studies that can give them

[1]The Foreign Education Bill pending before the Parliament is expected to bring huge foreign investment to help raise the ratio of college going students from the current 12 percent of all school graduates entering college to 30 percent by 2020 (Jhingan 2010).

employment; either that or in building employability. Our policies toward education and youth have begun to show this bias already.

Of course, keeping them employed has a huge side benefit too: this way the youth can be kept out of harm's way. The Prime Minister's response, during that famous summer of discontent in Kashmir when youth came out to pelt stones at the police day after day for months, was to suggest to the Chief Minister to shoot jobs rather than bullets as a means of crowd control. Lull your conscience, he seemed to be telling the youth; put your Azadi aspirations to sleep; bid sweet dreams to participation in the democracy; and listen to our lullabies of a corporatized world with employment for all (see Figure 3.2).

So, not only is employment and growth seen as the ticket to the country's rise to a global superpower, but also as the counter to all the insurgencies in the country. While no one can deny that livelihood skills and opportunities are a critical need for young people, they also need other skills so that they are able to discover their potential, make their own life choices, and work well with others. Unfortunately, mainstream education in India limits itself to polishing one facet of youth—how to become a good worker, and ignores all the current and future roles of a good friend, child, parent, sibling, or citizen. Recognizing this, the National Curriculum Framework 2005 for school education states that "learning has become an isolated activity which does not encourage children to link knowledge with their lives in any organic or vital way" and "the future of the child has taken center stage to the near exclusion of the child's present" (NCERT 2005).

Figure 3.2: Panacea for All Evils

Source: Authors.

We have talked of this balance between the Now and Future in Chapter 1. The Framework goes on to suggest that pedagogic practices must also be alert to promoting participation, building self-confidence and critical awareness, amongst others.

Education cannot merely be a response to market needs. Technical skills may increase knowledge but without leadership and relationship skills and even more importantly without the underlying values of justice, peace, and compassion, this knowledge can become self-serving and counter-productive. For example, doctors without ethics, empathy, and compassion can do more long-term damage than good—even though they may have an excellent academic record. As Professor K. S. Jacob of Christian Medical College, Vellore, observes: The current medical curriculum with

> its science-only focus make physicians short sighted with little understanding of long-term solutions to common diseases.... The art of medicine is based on an understanding of human nature, the cultural context and social expectations. Issues like stigma attached to certain diseases, such as TB and HIV have a huge impact on seeking medical help and compliance with treatment. Pure biological strategies adopting only medication do not have the desired effect. (Jacob 2010, p. 10)

Instead, effective medicine demands an understanding of the social, psychological, and cultural issues concerning the patient. This lacuna is not only because of curriculum concerns, but also due to a lack of infrastructure, funding for teachers, and training. Polishing one (vocational) facet of a rough diamond will only turn it into a mirror. And then why do we wonder that young people have become so narcissistic and self-centered?

The parallel of the economistic approach outlined above to the Women In Development (WID) approach is striking. Like the economistic approach that views young people as a potential demographic dividend, the WID approach advocated by United States Agency for International Development (USAID) in the seventies argued that women, who constitute 50 percent of the population, are an untapped resource who can provide an economic contribution to development. Instead of looking at their full range of rights, women were looked at as capital to be tapped. Efforts were, therefore, made to train women and include them in development processes (Moser 1993). While these efforts did draw women into the workforce and gave them opportunities to earn a livelihood, they did not necessarily improve the quality of their lives.

Because these efforts viewed women purely through an economistic lens, they failed to address the systemic social and cultural issues that led to unequal social relations between men and women. Their other roles were ignored. Even in the organized sector, women continued to get lower paid jobs and faced exploitation at the workplace. We in the youth development sector need to learn from the experiences of the early years of women's development programs and prevent repeating the same mistakes. Young people cannot be reduced to "human capital." We cannot afford to ignore the ocean within them.

ARE YOUNG PEOPLE A PROBLEM THAT NEEDS TO BE ADDRESSED?

A second set of policymakers views young people as the *client group for development interventions*. Their strategies consist of interventions where young people are often seen as *the problem* that needs to be solved. Young people are typically characterized as lacking something—health, education, peace of mind, law, and order—that makes them potentially destructive members of society. They are painted as substance abusers, petty criminals, brainwashed *jehadi*s, mercenary fighters, or sexual offenders. The interventions seek to eliminate this deficit. Several NGOs as well as government departments run programs for young people with the objective of eliminating such abuses and violations of law and order perpetrated by this group. In all these interventions, young people are often the recipients of services provided without necessarily playing any role in designing the intervention or the service.

Here again, there are striking parallels with strategies adopted by government programs and international aid agencies working supposedly for "women's development." In fact, women became a client group when governments and aid agencies realized that they could reduce population growth and infant mortality by targeting women. Women's development was not the goal. Rather women were seen only as the means to achieve other development goals. Similarly, young people are often targeted by welfare programs aimed at reducing illiteracy, substance abuse, HIV/AIDS, or unemployment rates. While all these interventions are necessary for an "affected" sector of young people, youth development, however, is not the priority.

CAN YOUTH BE VIEWED AS INSTRUMENTS FOR SOCIAL CHANGE?

This strategy views young people as valuable resources in the form of community workers, volunteers, or peer educators who can contribute their time, energy, skills, and labor toward achieving development goals. In this strategy, the focus has shifted significantly from eliminating youth *deficits* to supporting youth *assets*. These programs provide young people with opportunities that enable them to contribute to society. However, once again the objective of these programs is the achievement of development goals, rather than addressing the specific needs of young people. Women's development programs have also seen women as instruments of change in their community roles. More and more development programs target women and youth as community workers for reaching their development goals.

There are a range of institutions that employ this strategy and have harnessed youth energy to reach their goals. Depending on the nature of the organization, there are three broad ways of youth engagement: *(a)* as service providers and community development workers, *(b)* as foot soldiers for religious and social causes, *(c)* as a vote/support bank and mobilization force for political parties and mass movements. Sometimes, organizations also use a combination of these methods, depending on their ideology and sectoral leaning. Let's look at some of the specific instances of these different sub-strategies.

Youth ministry

For the government, young people have always been a valuable resource in the grand project of nation building. The Ministry of Youth Affairs implements a host of national youth service programs that pursue the twin objectives of character building and nation building. Among these, are the flagship programs of the Nehru Yuva Kendra Sangathan (NYKS) and the National Service Scheme (NSS), in addition to the Bharat Scouts and Guides, the Rashtriya Sadhbavana Yojana, the National Integration Scheme, and the National Service Volunteer Scheme. However, as highlighted in Chapter 1, the priority in practice is clearly on sports (and the national prestige that comes with it) rather than youth development. The lopsided focus on the Commonwealth Games 2010 is a case in point.

The National Youth Policy 2003 recognizes the contribution that youth can make to the growth and well-being of the community and seeks to promote youth volunteerism and leadership in the development of communities. It mentions the need to develop the qualities of citizenship, but locates this need in the context of community service and commitment to the goals of development programs (Articles 4.2 and 4.6, "National Youth Policy 2003," http://www.youth-policy.com/policies/ (downloaded on November 7, 2012). Although it sees the need for "individual character building," the thrust is clearly on community development.

Even the national youth service programs that claim to be for the development of young people have, in fact, more to do with community development—as indicated in the term "service"—rather than the "needs" of the young volunteers. By the term "needs," we refer largely to the learning and self-development opportunities that don't necessarily get foregrounded in these initiatives. Since the objective is nation building, the individual's self-development is not given as much attention.

The NYKS, for example, was launched in 1972 to give rural non-student youth the opportunity to engage in social and community development. There are approximately 50,000 *kendras* (centers) across the country today that encourage the development of youth clubs to promote awareness of community issues and participate in a variety of development projects.

The National Service Scheme (NSS) was formed in 1969 and designed to encourage university students to engage in volunteer work for poverty reduction and rural development. Its objective is student development through community service. Youth participants in the other programs contribute to emergency relief, tree plantation drives, blood donation drives, HIV/AIDS awareness campaigns, etc. All these programs have a huge outreach and could become great platforms for building leadership skills of young people that would enable them to discover their own potential and impact their communities even after the program is over. As of now, however, the focus is clearly on community service. This is seen as a duty of the young—what the country wants from them. And because the schemes don't look out for what the youth want, they are not very attractive to youth and hardly draw on their real passions and energy like the Independence movement did.

Religious organizations

A religious revival of sorts seems to have gripped the world, brought on possibly by the largely Christian West taking on the "Islamic" majority countries post 9/11. A flagging story has got wind in its sails again.

Religious organizations in India, too, have been very successful in mobilizing and engaging youth. The big advantage they have over, say an NGO or the government trying to inspire young people on social issues, is the legitimacy they are given by family structures. Young people are able to participate in religious processes with complete support of their parents who may otherwise not be as willing to let their children take part in social action. Religious organizations have the added advantage of providing young people a "safe" space in which to meet other like-minded youth.

For instance, youth groups in the Church offer a mix of action and intermingling, through celebrations, career and marriage counseling services and social service (voluntary work, funeral services for the deprived, fund-raising in times of calamities). Christian Student movements like All India Christian Students' Federation and Student Christian Movement of India (SCMI) also organize college students in a big way and engage them in social action.

The Rashtriya Swayamsevak Sangh (RSS) has extremely well-organized programs for mobilization and action based on their ideology of Hindutva. The primary means of mobilization here is through attracting youth to *shakhas* (basic unit) and *sangh* schools (RSS schools). The Shakha Milans have a combination of physical, mental, and spiritual development activities including sports, physical exercise, group discussions, speeches, songs, and reading of texts written by the leaders. It is to be noted that the regular and daily attendance of the *shakha* is a design masterstroke of the *sarvsangchalak* (head facilitator) as it keeps alive the philosophy of the Sangh amidst the routine of daily life.

While religious organizations may have done outstanding community work and helped to improve the living conditions of the poor, young participants remain within predefined ideological frameworks and do not have the space to explore their own values or form their own stances. We are not talking here of young people questioning faith; rather about them being encouraged to ask the right questions. This practice, if allowed, can only deepen their faith. Reason gives the mind a cloak in which to clothe the naked feelings aroused by faith.

Political organizations

All major political parties have youth wings and while the primary motivation is obviously to build support for their politics and as a vote bank, each of them also claim to provide opportunities for social action. The new "youth strategy" launched by Rahul Gandhi to strengthen the

Congress party by opening and democratizing the Indian Youth Congress has attracted many young people and swelled its membership to nearly 10 million. The goal of the transformation efforts was to create "holistic leaders and strengthen moral leadership" according to G. K. Jayaram, the consultant and facilitator for this process. Young leaders, representing different socioeconomic groups, are selected through a talent search and then attend a training course that covers a range of issues including responsibilities of office bearers, dealing with the media, and campaigning for the party. During the lead-up to elections, members are at the frontline of the campaign, holding public meetings, *padyatras* (journeys on foot) and panchayat conventions in villages, talking about local issues like corruption, lack of proper schools, illegal construction, National Rural Employment Guarantee Act (NREGA) implementation, etc. Open elections to the Indian Youth Congress (IYC) have also ensured that young people get elected as office bearers based on their own merit instead of kinship or influence. However, there have also been several conflicts between the old guard and the new kids on the block who are also eyeing positions of power. As Pratap Bhanu Mehta commented, "the issue isn't who's coming into politics. The issue is what happens *after* they enter politics" (cited in Jeelani 2011). The performance of the young parliamentarians has been the biggest disappointment in recent years. While in the seventies young people in politics took a stand and had a political identity, today's politics has been professionalized and produces politicians who are wary of taking a stand on controversial issues (ibid.). While the entry of youth into politics may be increasing minimally in recent times, one of the biggest worries remains the issue of dynasty politics. Sons and daughters of existing politicians have entered politics almost always into the same party as their parents. They hold very similar worldviews and represent the same constituencies. Democracy Connect is an initiative that is trying to address this issue. It works with future members of parliament who are currently active in the youth wings of their party and trains them to deal with policy issues so that "political processes shift from opportunistic, short-term, local patronage to more long-term, responsible legislation and development" (http://india.ashoka.org/fellow/nisha-prabha-tewari).

The youth wing of the BJP—the Bharatiya Janata Yuva Morcha (BJYM)—has organized campaigns and protests on several issues raised by the BJP in its role as the opposition party. These issues include corruption, specifically bringing back Indian black money in Swiss banks, price rise of essential commodities and services, protection of Indian students in Australia and India's soft approach on Pakistan and terrorism.

The Students Federation of India (SFI) is linked to the Communist Party of India (Marxist) (CPI[M]). It is one of the biggest student organizations with a membership of 4.2 million. It organizes lectures for students on political issues, such as the Palestine question, America's war on Afghanistan, the Mumbai terror attacks, etc., where students can build their perspectives, voice their opinions, and advocate for justice. Prominent in student politics, especially in Kerala, West Bengal, and Tripura, it has been used as a training ground and stepping stone for several college students to enter mainstream politics.

NGOs and social movements

There are also many NGOs that mobilize and include youth in their programs *as volunteers and community workers to achieve their social goals*. Some of them, for example, have youth groups or *yuva manchs* that take on roles such as outreach, mobilization, and peer education to address the issue that the organization is working on. While these provide leadership opportunities to young people, it is necessary to look at the nature of youth participation in these programs. Are young people involved in the design, planning, and decision-making roles or do they simply implement predetermined tasks? How do these roles enhance their leadership skills, their ability to think for themselves, and make informed choices? How do young people learn and build leadership and relating skills? At the same time, there is no denying the "success" these programs may have achieved in terms of reducing poverty, illiteracy, or environmental degradation. For example, the Centre of Science and Environment has launched the Green School Program that enables students to become environment managers and impact environmental issues around their schools. Using a simple audit map and a do-it-yourself handbook on how to audit the management of water, air, energy, waste, and land within school premises, the program has drawn students and teachers out of classrooms to count, weigh, measure, explore, and analyze the school environment. In schools where resources are scarce, the environment audit conducted as part of the Green School's Program, focuses on ensuring that basic needs are met; in schools where there is plenty, the audit helps prevent wastage. Over a two-year period (2007–2008) the project found a startling improvement in conservation practices. An example was increasing the actual rainfall harvested from 3 percent to 70 percent (Perold 2009). It would be safe to surmise that there might have been a significant impact on the environmental awareness of students and teachers and knowledge gained from experience and action, rather than books and lectures. And yet, although there may be participation by young people, it is still within the boundaries defined by someone else. While the learning about the environment (in the Green School project) is significant, the opportunity of processing how the environment impacts the young person is missed.

Movements like the Narmada Bachao Andolan and the recent India Against Corruption group have also mobilized the young in large numbers. Some journalists have called the Ram Lila Maidan an open school of democracy. And we at Pravah can vouch for the large number of youth leaders that have come out of the Narmada Andolan and joined the development sector. So, while these movements have had rub-off benefits on young people's character and the Self, these moments when society is seeping into their young hearts and changing them forever have not been processed at all. Psychological transformation was not the cause they were fighting for, say activists well connected to the core of the Andolan; on the other hand the young people who joined the movement owed a debt to the poor villagers in Maharashtra and Madhya Pradesh, and they joined the core team in fighting the lopsided development model being thrust upon the country. Likewise, corruption was the core issue at the Ram Lila grounds and getting the government to accept the demands and concerns around the Lokpal Bill was of paramount interest to the mobilizers; their presumption and clear expectation was that when someone entered the grounds they left behind every other identity search they might be on. The agenda had been set; the young person's agency was limited to choosing whether you were with India Against Corruption or against them.

Although there are several excellent examples of institutions using the Youth for Development strategy to achieve development goals, it is not entirely without controversy. Who, for example, defines this goal and the means to reach this goal? Are young people being used to further an agenda determined by adults?

History is replete with examples of young people acting as foot soldiers for a cause. The starkest example is the recruitment of young people by extremists to fight for an ideological cause, often in the name of wresting justice. There are villages today in Odisha where there are no young males to be found, since they have been cajoled or coerced into the Naxal movement or the Salwa Judum. Also, consider the brainwashing done in the name of religion or other causes that make young people go against the basic evolutionary instinct of survival. The practice of suicide bombing, started by the Liberation Tigers of Tamil Eelam (LTTE) in the eighties has only strengthened in the last two decades. We do not bat an eyelid any more at the news of another suicide bomber blowing himself/herself up.

If this might seem an extreme example of instrumentalizing young people, we can cite many others. Politicians and local leaders use youth as vote banks and free labor to campaign for their parties and mobilize support. Many college campuses have student wings of major political parties that spread the party message among the student community, fight elections, and recruit new members. However, most of them do not have any real powers in the running of their colleges (see Figure 3.3). To prevent this manipulation of young people, we, at Pravah, have developed a more youth-centric approach. We turn to this lens finally to outline a fourth way of viewing young people that we hope to convince more and more navigators to use. Even while we facilitate what a young volunteer can contribute to the world, this approach foregrounds what the world contributes to the volunteer.

Figure 3.3: Youth *for* Development

Source: Authors.

CAN'T WE LOOK AT A MORE YOUTH-CENTRIC APPROACH? CAN WE GET THE YOUNG PEOPLE TO PAINT THEMSELVES INTO THE PICTURE?

Youth-centric development refers to processes that are based on the young person's needs in their special stage of development and to using social action for building the leadership potential of youth (Patel 2006) to be able to fulfill these needs. It recognizes the urgent requirement to engage with youth as individuals with unique identities and a desire to learn, explore and understand their own potential as active citizens (see Figure 3.4). The aim or the cause is the young person himself/herself and his/her development. Youth-centric strategies view the young person as a partner in addressing development problems and impacting the world but at the same time studying the impact of the world on the young and nurturing their potential as change agents.

As we had mentioned in Chapter 1, the old knowledge monopolies of adults have been smashed by the advent of electronic media. If any generation gap exists between adults and the young, it is not the gap of

Figure 3.4: Youth-centric Development

Source: Authors.

knowledge but rather the gap of application. Here we mean experiences that allow young people to internalize concepts by learning from their mistakes and successes. Creating safe, youth-led spaces where they can take the journey of the self to society and back is what this fourth strategy is all about. This strategy requires an investment in the development of the young person and ensures that they are being prepared for citizenship roles that will continue beyond their engagement with the organization or movement. It looks at social action as an education methodology, a pedagogic tool for teaching the young about themselves. There are not too many organizations that engage youth from this perspective.

Our journeys at Pravah involve a transformation (in the Self and Society) from "me" to "we," through a process of building self-awareness and engagement with social issues. Through this process, youth enable themselves to lead citizenship action, become deeply self aware, and bring about social change. Formed in 1993, following the demolition of the Babri Masjid, the founders of Pravah realized that the education system does not prepare young people with skills, values, and attitudes needed to become socially responsible decision-makers. Though our voyage started with the Self, in the first decade and a half of our work, we focused more on social issues. While building leadership was of essence, it was done through action projects and volunteering with other NGOs.

"Before, I knew when something was wrong, but didn't know what to do. Now I know how to address it, how to create dialogue about it."

Nitin, Std. XI, Ramjas School

In the last couple of years, while keeping the future objective of creating a cadre of powerful decision-makers at the back of our mind, we have essentially begun to foreground the identity formation stage of the young person. For this, we have concentrated on creating a space that young people can own, where they are in charge, where they experiment with creating impact in the world and, in turn, let the world impact their Selves. While the individual is important, we don't create personal learning voyages for each one. We believe that every young person has to own their learning. They are the navigators and the crew for their voyage of self-discovery. Pravah facilitators provide them the safe space in the vast ocean run by adult rules to play and experiment and learn; that is, we give them the space to become sea-worthy, ready for the voyage they will undertake and the ones they are already on. By shifting our focus from the individual to a context/womb that can organically spawn youth leadership through experiential reflection, we have honored our hypothesis of Chapter 1 by not creating another cloistered classroom "teaching" social issues, instead the space lets them take initiative to share leadership and explore themselves. In this space, we lightly build on that all-important connection between Self and societal interests. The space offers young people a number of approaches that include self-exploration, workshops, feedback, analysis, reflection, citizenship education, opportunities for exposure to social issues through volunteering, rural camps, action projects and campaigns, mentoring and internships. We also facilitate young social entrepreneurs to start up their own social change initiatives. A more detailed analysis of our experiments with youth (including how the all-critical womb, a space that organically gives birth to leadership, can be set up) is outlined in Chapter 5. In the next chapter, we try to provide a compelling argument for society to legimitize and promote many more such experiential capacity-building spaces for the young.

To end this chapter, we provide examples of other organizations that believe in youth-centric development. They may not all be looking at youth as an identity-formation phase but they do certainly believe, like us, that at this stage society has as much to contribute to the young person as the latter needs to give to society. Youth leadership capacity building forms a key part of their project. This is not an exhaustive list. Instead we have chosen a few to illustrate different ways organizations are adopting a youth-centric approach in their work.

Box 3.1: PUKAR, Mumbai

PUKAR (Partners for Urban Knowledge Action and Research), Mumbai, is a member of Commutiny—The Youth collective, a design and policy group of 15 youth-centric organizations and individuals, incubated by Pravah and the Sir Ratan Tata Trust.

The Youth Fellowship, PUKAR's flagship project, is a unique knowledge initiative, which provides a space for the critical engagement of mostly marginalized youth. It uses research as a pedagogical, interventional, and advocacy tool to empower youth to negotiate the city and focuses on transformation processes of the youth, the community they work with, and the society at large. These Barefoot Researchers use the city itself as a learning lab to build new urban knowledge without the intermediary of a formal structure of learning that tends to otherwise distance them from their contexts. Most of their research topics are situated in their localities and anchored in their living experiences. This experiential learning exposes them to the existing hierarchies and social, cultural, and economic diversities of the world to which the learner/researcher belongs. Thus, the Barefoot Researchers gain the ability to reflect upon their own selves, learn to ask vital questions related to social practices and governance, challenge the prevalent wisdom to make arguments about their future, and become problem-solvers for the future of their cities. The format of group research helps to inculcate certain values necessary for sustaining an inclusive, participatory, democratic system of governance.

Rahul Mankar: A Barefoot Researcher

Hailing from suburban Kalyan, Rahul and his mixed group explored "friendship," a critical aspect of youth identity, through instruments of interviews and photographs. Their research revealed that prejudices about caste, religion, and economic status play a significant role in forming and sustaining friendships. The impact of the group research was felt strongly by every member. During a recent interview, Rahul said: "In addition to improving my communication skills, listening skills, and conflict resolution skills, the process helped me to change my attitude toward the diverse views of others, respecting those views and taught me to think out of the box for all issues touching my life."

Rahul also felt that he has learnt the importance of bringing about social change that must first start within him. Together with his group "Yaar" he is now engaged in an action project that he believes helps the youth as well as the larger societal structures.

For more information, please visit www.pukar.org.in

Source: Compiled by the authors from varioues sources.

Box 3.2: The YP Foundation, New Delhi

The YP Foundation (TYPF) promotes and protects young people's human rights by building leadership skills and strengthening youth-led initiatives and movements. It is led and run entirely by young people. Founded in 2002, TYPF supports and enables young people to create programs and influence policies in the areas of gender, sexuality, health, education, the arts and governance. TYPF supports young people between the ages of 13 and 28 through a year-long program to conceptualize, design, and implement community-based projects that challenge stereotypes, forge sustainable partnerships, and provide an opportunity for self-expression. Over the past nine years, TYPF has worked with 5,000 young people to set up over 200 projects in India, reaching out to more than 300,000 young people. The projects span a number of issues and groups, such as climate change, leadership training for young social entrepreneurs, ensuring access to non-formal education and health care for out-of-school children, life skills and mental health projects with in-school children, sexual reproductive health and rights awareness programs for peer educators, awareness programs on voter's rights, and support for young people and livelihood sustainability and arts education with young filmmakers, artists, and writers. The array of projects ensures that young people get a chance to get hands-on experience working with an issue they care about, enabling them to understand human rights and social justice issues and develop their leadership skills while doing something they enjoy. As a former team member described it, "This was my happy space." The organization believes and institutes a shared leadership model that contributes to the high levels of belonging and ownership at TYPF. The senior management team is collectively responsible for developing, mentoring, and building internal capacities. Six program divisions develop and host project ideas and train 350 volunteers each year to run and sustain the projects. One of the core values of TYPF is dynamic learning through reflection from action and vice versa. The evaluation mechanism at TYPF brings together all volunteers, staff, and board members every quarter for a series of brainstorming meetings during which they develop the mission and goals of each program division and review and evaluate each project. The core staff team changes every two years and the volunteer base rotates every year ensuring constant renewal and the influx of new ideas.

For more information please visit www.theypfoundation.org

Source: Compiled by the authors.

Box 3.3: Doosra Dashak, Rajasthan

Another example of this approach is Doosra Dashak which seeks to build capacities of young people in rural Rajasthan to engage with local issues, become advocates, and strengthen participatory democracy.

Doosra Dashak organizes residential camps for nonliterate youth and dropouts, as well as school students between the ages of 11–20. These camps focus on developing responsible citizens who can become contributing members of their communities. Besides providing an education tailored to the needs of marginalized youth, the curriculum includes areas that are typically neglected in mainstream curricula, such as sexual and reproductive health, leadership, relationships, and self-esteem.

Besides the camps, young people also have access to *ikhvelo*s (learning centers) and *vigyan kendra*s (science centers) set up by Doosra Dashak. These are centers for continuous and self-directed learning, where young people can read books and newspapers, experiment with science models, and develop a scientific approach. These centers are also used as venues for youth meetings and trainings on issues such as gender, panchayati raj, Right to Information (RTI), and health.

Doosra Dashak also provides opportunities for young people to take on leadership roles, develop their skills, and address social issues that impact their communities. This is done through the youth forums which are led by young people.

After the camps, younger adolescents get admitted in age-appropriate grades in their village school. They as well as the older participants return to their villages and start a youth forum, which assesses the development needs of the village and then comes up with an appropriate intervention to address this need. In Pali district, for example, where maternal and child health indicators were very poor, youth forum members started connecting the Auxiliary Nurse Midwives (ANMs) with the tribal communities so that tribal women and children could access health services. A recent survey shows improved health status in the district. Today, the local government contacts the youth forum whenever they want to organize a health camp. Young people have also used RTI to investigate the hoarding of grains by ration dealers during famine months. In Kishanganj block of Baran district, members of the youth forum coordinate campaigns and conduct social audits. They are also invited to train young people in other districts.

The youth forums send representatives to the *yuva shakti sangathan*, an apex group at the block level that assesses needs of young people and accordingly organizes and coordinates training sessions that enable youth to develop their skills as active citizens.

For more information, please visit www.doosradashak.in

Source: Compiled by the authors.

Box 3.4: The Bosco Institute, Guwahati

In order to make young people more resourceful and resilient, a number of projects in the North East of India work with young people to build the values of democracy, respect and a language of peace. The Bosco Institute, Guwahati, in collaboration with North Eastern Regional Youth Centre runs

Operation Shanti which is building a movement for peace with young people at the center. It builds capacities of young people to assist friends in their personal and social lives, and to assist victims of violence. With more young people opting for peace education, there is a greater willingness to talk "peace" and bring divided villages together.

> I now realize how important it is to see different situations from different perspectives and above all the need for reconciliation from thoughts like anger, fear.... I decided to help my community and people using all the knowledge I have about conflict resolution. I focused mainly on youth groups, allowing myself to help them to be aware of the crisis our community is going through.
>
> —Rebecca, Peace Educator, Manipur

Source: Compiled by the authors.

Box 3.5: YUVA, Mumbai

YUVA (Youth for Unity and Voluntary Action), Mumbai, has facilitated the formation of the Maharashtra Yuva Manch (MYM), a semi-political youth organization with a membership of around 9,000 across Maharashtra. Through their program, Anubhav Shiksha Kendra, young people who have not gone through a formal education system are helped to go through a graded process of three to five years to reflect, understand oneself better and also the world around oneself. The MYM is also pushing the youth manifesto and agenda among the political parties. YUVA has been particularly successful in facilitating youth in organizing themselves and acting on issues of entitlement and identity.

Source: Compiled by the authors.

Box 3.6: SAHER, Mumbai

This youth-led organization working with young people in Jogeshwari, Mumbai, and a partner of Pravah was set up by a group of friends affected by the Mumbai riots of 1993. One of their programs, Parwaaz aims at creating interactive spaces for youth from various backgrounds. College students go through a journey of self-exploration while learning collectively. It uses experiential learning to enable young people to explore their abilities and dreams, understand that there are multiple and diverse realities, learn to recognize and respect differences, develop skills to deal with conflicts, and build a sense of ownership and responsibility toward community resources and the environment.

For more information, please visit www.saher.org

Source: Compiled by the authors.

Box 3.7: Yuv Shakti, Ahmedabad

Janvikas initiated this youth development program in the three most-affected *taluka*s (blocks) of Panchmahal district, post the Gujarat riots of 2002. Developed as a long-term strategy to avoid recurrence of such incidents, this program empowers youth toward understanding themselves and social issues around them, besides enabling them to participate in village development and address the needs of young people and communities. The program emphasizes the importance of peace promotion and conflict transformation and addresses challenges of caste politics.

Source: Compiled by the authors.

Box 3.8: Thoughtshop Foundation, Kolkata

Thoughtshop Foundation develops youth facilitators who build youth resource cells (YRCs) in their neighborhoods. YRCs are envisioned as hubs for community development—enabling young people to achieve their potential and bring about positive social change. Young people are seen as partners in the process of social change rather than beneficiaries. The process builds ownership, responsibility, and sustainability.

YRCs work as spaces for healing and support for members, play a watchdog role in the neighborhood, act as change-makers introducing new ideas. They are spaces for self-discovery, learning opportunities and they help create positive social change specifically in their neighborhoods.

The program reaches out to young people from diverse religious, rural, peri-urban, and slum communities. Participants go through a journey that helps them explore themselves, learn life skills, build a connection with their neighborhoods and understand social challenges. It makes an impact at three levels: individual young people, youth groups, and communities.

At an individual level, young people explore their personal issues of identity, choice, values, and life goals. They get opportunities for self-development on teamwork, assertiveness, planning, and facilitation skills.

As a collective, young people learn to work as teams and slowly evolve into YRCs having a set of values, and functioning as independent youth organizations.

At the community level, YRCs demonstrate the role of youth in addressing community issues and address specific social challenges, such as gender inequality, domestic violence, child right violations, etc.

The program is structured through a year-long fellowship program involving weekly workshops, residential camps for YRC members, and social action projects in the community. It is implemented through a peer approach with young people from the fellowship program graduating to become youth trainers and peer counselors. Since many of the young people come from marginalized communities, the program primarily uses a wide range of pictorial tools and games, and other interactive techniques to assist peer facilitators initiate a dialogue at YRCs.

Voices of Young People from the YRCs

When I used to speak about my parents, the words would be accusatory. After joining this group and being part of these workshops I realized that there was a lot of anger in my heart still. I realized that I have to try and understand other people's point of view. Now I feel much lighter and happier. I am able to accept my parents as they are rather than blame them for what happened or trying to change them.

—Male, 18 years (abandoned by both parents in childhood), YRC Youth Voice (VIP Nagar, Urban slum settlement)

We have never mixed with other religions before because that is what we were told at home. But at the camp, I thought that they are all human beings like us. They have a god just like we do. We used to spend time together, eat together—it really felt very good.

—Female, 16 years, YRC Roshni (urban slum, Muslim girls group)

Now many young people approach me with their problems. One 16-year-old girl who was facing violence at her in-laws' place ran away and came back home. However, the "para" boycotted her and she felt completely isolated. She shared her problems with me and I could understand her pain. After all, even I had been treated badly by the community. I spent a lot of time with her listening to her and counselling her—sometimes even on the roadside. My mother was against this as she felt it might give me a bad name as well. Anyway, I didn't care about that. I slowly brought her to our group and introduced her to all the activities. She's a totally different person now! She is confident, self-assured, involved in the group's work and has found acceptance in the community as well.

—Peer Facilitator, Female, 20 years, YRC Jyoti

For more information, please visit thoughtshopfoundation.org

Box 3.9: Patang, Sambalpur

Patang, Odisha, was started in 2003 with a vision to create youth leadership in rural and semi-urban parts of western Odisha. The team consists of young people who started their journey as volunteers and today run programs and participate in all the organizational processes and decisions.

Patang's model creates an enabling environment and takes young people through an experiential learning process so that they can transform themselves and their communities. For example, volunteers with Patang's Pathmakers program participate in self-development and leadership camps and skill-building workshops. They also lead and participate in campaigns to highlight and spread awareness on different issues, such as the RTI, Gender Equality, and Appreciating Diversity. These campaigns enable young people to understand different perspectives and take stances on social issues that impact them. It also gives them an opportunity to demonstrate that they can make a difference. During the summer vacations, volunteers are placed with grassroots NGOs and movements across the country. These processes enable young people to get out of their comfort zone, analyze their attitudes, values, and stereotypes and also build their skills and confidence to challenge them.

Patang also builds skills in young people, so that they can assess the need of a community, design a viable intervention and implement it. The Squirrel program develops a cadre of volunteers at the community level by supporting young people to volunteer and work directly with the community. For example, volunteers have implemented projects on malaria prevention, construction of toilets, monitoring midday meals, promoting organic farming, and setting up community libraries, to name just a few.

The Anubhav Shiksha Kendra reaches out to children, adolescents, young people, teachers, parents, and the community and facilitates interaction, workshops, debates, and discussion. It is a space for learning outside the four walls of the school and coaching centers and is run by a core group of young people elected by the youth members. The core group designs and facilitates activities for youth members such as meetings, film screenings, theater workshops and action projects on RTI, food security, waste management, and gender discrimination.

A core component of the adolescent life skills curriculum is the social action project. The action project is always on an issue that is suggested by participants and is relevant to their lives. Designed by the participants, the action project provides participants an opportunity to apply what they have learned and experience the Self to Society connection by inspiring others and making a difference to a locally relevant social issue they care deeply about.

For further information, please visit www.patangindia.org

Source: Compiled by the authors.

Box 3.10: Manzil, New Delhi

Manzil is a youth empowerment and learning center in Khan Market, New Delhi, that provides opportunities and resources for young people to learn, teach, be creative, and see the world in new ways. It offers classes in Maths, English, Computers, Music, Painting, Dance, and Theater.

In contrast to the traditional classroom, in Manzil there is no hierarchy between teachers and learners. Rather than teachers providing the answers, students are expected to ask questions, think for themselves, and learn though experience and action. Students are encouraged to take on the role of a teacher and initiate classes of their own, based on the belief that everyone is both a learner and a teacher.

Manzil also fosters opportunities for young people to express themselves outside the classroom. For example, music has become a popular medium of expression, and students have created their own bands that are invited to perform at various events. They write their own lyrics that express their thoughts and feelings and also explore different kinds of music that they would not hear ordinarily. Theater is another medium that has attracted many young people. However, theater is not viewed as a product to be put up on stage or as a potential profession for young people. Instead theater is treated as a pedagogic tool—a "process of observing, exploring, revisiting and representing the various subtleties and shades of our inner and outer lives." Through various workshops, young people have acquired a more confident outlook, a reflective openness, and sensitivity to various issues, ideas, and relationships around them.

Exposure trips to other NGOs have been instrumental in providing insights that bridge the gap between textual information "taught" within the confines of syllabus and school, and the lived realities of flesh-and-blood people. As a result, Manzil students are stimulated into thinking and acting on issues that remain largely invisible or deliberately disconnected from our own lives and consciousness.

Most importantly, Manzil fosters compassion for those within and outside the community. This close-knit group provides opportunities to young people to understand how they may enrich themselves and create lasting relationships with their fellow community members. Former Manzil students often return to teach classes and serve as a testament to the educational system at Manzil.

For more information, please visit www.manzil.in

Source: Compiled by the authors.

To summarize the fourth lens strategy of youth-centric development, the output is envisaged as the young person herself and not the advancement of a cause. The processes used allow for reflection, feedback, analysis, identity explorations, and capacity building so that the young person gains skills not only in how to intervene in a systemic way but also in mastery over the Self. Issues and social change are not the only focus, personal and group journeys are as critical.

CHAPTER HIGHLIGHTS

As a nation we seem to have adopted four broad strategies to engage the 330 million young Indians who form 40 percent of our population. The primary lens with which our policymakers seem to be viewing this diverse group is economic. Our education system is geared toward this and a huge investment in training young people for vocations is being planned as a way to ensure their successful entry into the job market. There are also those who look at young people as a client group for development interventions that seek to address and eliminate problems of this group, such as the lack of skills, health, education, livelihoods. The third strategy prevalent among many NGOs as well as the government, views young people as instruments of change—as volunteers who can contribute their time, energy, skills, and labor toward achieving development goals. From our perspective, a more youth-centric strategy (in contrast to youth *for* development), is required which emphasizes the identity-formation stage of youth processes, and action in the world is geared to build youth leadership. It also recognizes that the personal transformation of the young person is as critical as the societal transformation they can bring about. A few organizations using this broad approach were showcased to highlight the approaches used by navigators who view youth through the youth-centric lens.

In the next chapter, we examine why it is so important for more youth-centric strategies to be adopted rather than looking at youth from the other three lenses.

4

Why Are Youth-centric Spaces So Critical?*

Having outlined in the previous chapter the different lenses that have inspired various navigators of youth policy, we now turn to our central reason for writing this book. In this chapter, based on our research on the youth scene in India since the forties, we try to provide a compelling answer to the question: why do more organizations with large constituencies of young people need to adopt youth-centric processes? We argue that not only will this generate more systemic and long-term thinking youth leadership, but also a more vibrant, equal, and just society.

"Where are you? *Kahan ho abhi?*"

Since mobile technology and in particular the hand phone, this intrusive question has become a starting point in many mobile conversations. This question, we believe, originates from a primal human need to place people in a context. In the times of the landline it was easy to picture where the other person was. And before the telephone, all conversations took place face to face with both parties present in the same space. Spaces like home, school, office, playing field, etc., have always added meaning to human existence. The rules, by which these spaces are governed, therefore, become critical while making choices about whether one wants to enter or exit (in case there is such an option) the space.

For young people spaces have a defining influence. In Chapter 1, we outlined Karl Mannheim's hypothesis that young people are the children of their times. While he was referring to defining historical events that occur during a young person's impressionable years, such as the World

*This section owes a lot of the concepts to an article called "Reviving the Fifth Space," written in 2008 (unpublished paper) by Arjun Shekhar.

Wars or India's Freedom Movement, the theory can be extended to include spaces as well. It is a well-accepted fact that the rules governing a family, a school, or one's friends circle typically shape a young person's identity in some definitive way.

Social geography is often crucial to youth subcultures because the networks of power and the struggles for meaning creation and expression are particularly visible through their spatial orientation (Varner 2007).

Or put another way, the world is owned and run by adults, and the young know they have to wait their turn to sail the big boat. For most spaces, the rules have been created by adults and the young are expected to follow these without questioning them. So, is it any wonder that youth are forever on the lookout for new spaces to hang out at together? A place where they can let their hair down. A safe haven they can call their own. A sanctuary where they can be themselves and not be constantly judged. Why are such spaces so important for young people (see Figure 4.1)?

Figure 4.1: Youth in Search of Hangout Spaces

Source: Authors.

WHICH SPACES DOES SOCIETY LEGITIMIZE FOR YOUNG PEOPLE?

Traditionally, since Independence, in both urban and rural India, young people have occupied four spaces that have been socially sanctioned by the elders.

The *first* is, of course, the *home*. The family, unlike in the West, still remains an important space in the mindscape of Indian youth, as a 2009 study by CSDS revealed (De Souza et al. 2009). According to this study, 88 percent of young people would like to bring up their children exactly or mostly like they were brought up. That's a huge vindication for the much touted family values of our culture. Additionally, 75 percent of the young people interviewed believe parental authority should be strong or very strong. Further proof, if any was needed, of this reverence of the family in India can be found in the number of young people who would let their parents choose their spouse. This number is as high as 60 percent, a very substantial figure considering the increase in love marriages among youth icons on and off screen and the consequent supposed "erosion" of parental authority in the institution of marriage. Moreover, we suspect, though we don't have hard statistics to prove it, that a similar number of young folks would cede the choice of their careers (in cases where such choices exist) to their parents, typically their fathers. Thus, the findings of

Figure 4.2: The 1st Space—The Family

Source: Authors.

the CSDS survey remind us how significant the family space is to the young people of India (see Figure 4.2).

The *second* space legitimized by society today for youth is *career* or *an institution* (school/college/vocational course) that prepares them for one. In fact, in the heyday of India shining, this space has grown disproportionately at the cost of the others. We have already spoken about the government and corporate thrust to promote "productivity" in an effort to reap the demographic dividend. Employment and careers have certainly become critical areas of concern for young people. The CSDS study reveals that students and unemployed youth tend to report very high levels of anxiety. Twenty-seven percent of the respondents considered unemployment to be the biggest problem facing the country and felt the creation and guarantee of employment should be the first priority of the nation (see Figure 4.3).

The *third* space where youth spend their time can be loosely termed *leisure and lifestyle*. Here young people sometimes take on the role of actors, though mostly they make up the rank of spectators. In this space, we have included sports, the performing arts, religious/cultural occasions, and consumption spaces like markets and restaurants (see Figure 4.4).

An interesting case study of a mall in Hyderabad from the CSDS survey brings out how this space is being used as a hangout in an increasingly consumerist India.

Figure 4.3: The 2nd Space—Careers and Career-based Education

Source: Authors.

Figure 4.4: The 3rd Space—Leisure and Lifestyle

Source: Authors.

Box 4.1: Excerpt from "Youth and the Entertainment Mall: A Study of Prasad's Imax in Hyderabad"
By C. Ramachandraiah

> Many people go through the mall, window-shopping popular brands but very few people shop in the Imax. The Imax is a place for strolling and hanging around where a large number of visitors cannot exactly be considered as consumers because they don't buy anything. But they are consuming an experience. Many find it a "great place to hang out with friends." They are in the mall to access and enjoy the ambient mood of pleasure, freedom and safety.
>
> For the youth ... the Imax provides a space for enjoying a consumption experience, both real and imaginary: a sense of feeling free, shedding inhibitions, being in a world of their own, free from the social mores and gaze of the elders.

Source: De Souza et al. 2009.

Marketplaces were always a draw for the young but combined with free air-conditioning, movies, and fast food, the young are attracted to a mall like a horde of bees to a valley of flowers in full bloom. The third space of leisure and lifestyle is a loose bunch of attractions tied up in a somewhat unruly looking bouquet, and yet it serves the purpose of separating this experience from that of any other space (see Box 4.2).

Box 4.2: Electronic Media in the 3rd Space

A highlight that we need to take note of from the CSDS study (De Souza et al. 2009) is that watching television is an important leisure activity for young people. While the statistics behind this statement are not revealed, the figures of Internet usage are outlined. Even here the total average time of Internet usage is not given but the digital divide is clearly defined. The CSDS study reveals that 10 percent of the youth surveyed use the Internet mostly for emailing, chatting, and downloading information. One-third of these are in cities; one-fifth in small towns; and less than 10 percent in villages. There is also a big variation between usage among young people depending on their socioeconomic status and location: 38 percent of young people using the Internet belonged to higher socioeconomic status and only 1 percent belonged to a low economic status. While acknowledging the existence of the digital divide, we would still like to note that the Internet does seem to take up a substantial amount of leisure time for at least urban, wired youth and it's growing and may reach the USA statistic cited earlier (of average 1 hour 20 minutes of entertainment-related surfing by youth in a weekend) within a couple of years. It is important to note that the use of social networking sites in the urban milieu overlaps not only with the friends space but also the Active Citizenship space, considering the cyber activism that is in vogue today. The India Against Corruption movement and many others have mobilized young people in large numbers through these sites.

Source: Compiled by the authors.

The *fourth*, and undisputedly the most attractive space for young people, is not necessarily a space in the geographical meaning of the term, rather, it is a space in the young person's head or more precisely it is the time they spend with their *friends* (see Figure 4.5). All young people, in differing degrees, seek out the company of somebody they can bare their soul to, somebody who makes no judgments about their journey, somebody who can also help interpret the meaning of the journey—as a co-traveler, who is in the same boat as them. According to J. Krishnamurti, life is all about relating to others. He must have had the young in mind when he said this because most young people consider life without friends as a kind of a death sentence (see Box 4.3).

Figure 4.5: The 4th Space—Friends

Source: Authors.

Box 4.3: Cross-border Friendships

Though most young people may cite friendship as the most nourishing space of all, the CSDS study (in the rubric on Trust and Circles of Belonging) clearly indicates that young people still live on cultural islands, that is, most of their friends are from the same religion, caste, and gender. *Social borders are quite strong, and border crossings are infrequent.* Twenty-seven percent had no friends across the border and 21 percent crossed the border only occasionally. Having friends of the opposite sex is an option for only half the youth, and in sharp contrast to the forties, more than half do not have friends from other religions.

Not surprisingly, the study also reveals that for most youth, the "inner circle of trust" consists largely of those who are one's friends, relatives, neighbors, and those from one's own caste. *The question to be addressed is whether these findings are a reflection of conservative mores and/or a result of the lack of opportunity for interaction. In a situation of greater opportunity, would this conservatism hold people back from making friends across the border?* Our experience at Pravah indicates that this would not be the case and, in fact, young people look forward to spaces that enable them to engage with others across gender, religion, and caste borders.

Source: De Souza et al. 2009.

We feel that it is mostly in the above four spaces that young Indians today divide their time and energy, put in efforts, and spend their resources. Their virtual and real explorations chart out these spaces in their ocean but are also limited to it; that is to say, we believe these four spaces define almost their entire ocean.

IS THERE A 5TH SPACE?

Some commentators have begun to call the space of "Active Citizenship" as the 5th Space (see Figure 4.6). A small minority of young people hang out here, while others (as was seen in the anticorruption movement) pass through it like a floating population of migrant labor when sufficiently emotional issues and causes affecting them personally are raised. To determine whether "Active Citizenship" qualifies to be called a 5th Space, let's try to understand what this term has come to mean now and the changes this space has undergone over the past 70 years.

Unfortunately, that's easier said than done. Definitions range from constitutional to conversational. The former speaks of membership of the nation and its attendant rights, duties, and responsibilities enshrined in the Constitution. The latter refers to the countless *charcha*s (debates) about change over a *chai* that we all engage in as a means of addressing our concerns about the state of the world.

Wilfred Carr (2008) claims that it is better to treat citizenship as an "essentially contested concept"; to define it would reduce it to mere words and citizenship is so much more than that. We agree with Carr and take his reluctance at defining Active Citizenship a step further by declaring that the debate on what it is, is in itself an act of Active Citizenship. A definition would only dilute the concept by presenting an answer where questions should rule.

Without a formal definition, sometimes we can rely on experiences to give us the words we require.

Figure 4.6: The 5th Space: Self to Society

Source: Authors.

In the current context, the term has been mostly reduced to the experience of volunteering. Young people with a conscience or with inspiring guardians get attached to various causes in their spare time. They have short bursts of engagement with common spaces during lulls in the other four spaces. But there was a time in India's history when Active Citizenship took on equal priority; it was as important as, if not more than, the other spaces.

We spoke of the freedom movement in Chapter 2. There is no doubt that it was one of the greatest groundswell of Active Citizenship ever witnessed in this country. The movement drew in youth in a rainbow of ways. Millions of invisible young hands shared ideals and common spaces with a vibrant energy that overthrew an empire. Let's explore this upsurge of Active Citizenship a bit deeper. It was the most sustained effort by a large number of young people over a long period, which was legitimized by society—not just legitimized but, in fact, youth were encouraged to hitch their personal star to the common good. Before we settle on a broad understanding of what the 5th Space is, let's look at the reasons behind this groundswell of engagement with the Independence movement of India.

HOW DID THE INDEPENDENCE MOVEMENT MANAGE TO ATTRACT SO MANY YOUNG PEOPLE OVER SUCH A LONG PERIOD, THAT TOO AT THE COST OF PERSONAL GOALS?

In an attempt to find answers to this question, we conducted primary research amongst a sample of the youth of the forties[1] and also went through more than 50 oral transcripts of young people in the decade before Independence (see Annexures 3 and 4 for further details). Our study of the oral transcripts, contemporary literature, and secondary data (Bose 1982; Chattopadhyay 1987; Joshi 1972; Ray et al. 1984; Sarkar 1973) reveals an interesting trend that took place on the ground. Describing the growth of the student movement, R. Varma, President of the All India Students Congress in 1948, said,

---

[1]We interviewed 30 octogenarians who had been in their youth in the forties. Respondents were selected based on convenience and easy access. The sample, however, does have a fair gender balance and also consists of people who grew up in different parts of the country (urban and rural) and of varied education levels (see Annexure 4).

> [It] caught like wild fire, and spread into every nook and corner of this vast country of ours. There was a magic in its growth ... akin to a miracle, the way in which the student community responded to the call and spontaneously built up a vast and widespread organization.

Altbach (1970) reinforces these observations when he comments that by 1938,

> Indian colleges were highly politicized and students were involved in a variety of protest activities. There were strikes against college authorities almost weekly all over India. Thousands served short jail sentences for their part in the struggle, many left college to work in the nationalist and labor movements or Gandhian social service projects.

According to Altbach, about 10 percent of the student population in India (approximately 15,000 students) was involved in the daily organizational work of the Quit India Movement alone.

Why did so many young people from the mainstream jump into social action during those days? No one ordered them to be there. There weren't any concrete promises made. Neither was there any immediate self-interest. Indeed there were hardships, deprivations, and as we said before, in many cases, huge sacrifices.

Highlighting generational change, Karl Mannheim (1952) (as quoted earlier) proposed that *the context of the times* influences Active Citizenship among young people. This is definitely true for the youth of the forties who lived in the heady years leading up to Independence. As Mr Lal, one of the octogenarian respondents, points out, "Our generation was special because it was shaped by the cataclysmic events of the times—the Freedom Movement, World War II, Partition." Others of his generation recalled the Bengal Famine and communal riots as turning points for them. These events created the context for an entire generation of youth, giving them the exposure and opportunities to take up responsibilities, learn leadership skills, and make a difference. The magnitude of these events and the psychological appeal would have made it very difficult for them to stay aloof.

The difference between the Independence movement and the anticorruption movements of the seventies and 2011 is basically of scale, depth, and longevity. We believe the Independence movement has many lessons to teach us, one of the central ones being that it comprised a plethora of decentralized and *sustained social actions led by youth* (a few examples of this were seen during the Jai Prakash Narain (JP) movement of the seventies too, but it were JP who was in complete charge as was

Anna Hazare during the 2011 anticorruption crusade). The students' response to the Bengal Famine and the communal riots is a case in point (see Boxes 4.4 and 4.5). There were no big names on display here; the students took charge of the operation.

Box 4.4: Youth Responses to the Bengal Famine

For appeal to the student community.... *"Go and save at least one life. If you cannot do that, then slave with the stricken peasantry to reap the harvest. We cannot sit with folded hands"* (Secretary, Bengal Provincial Students Federation). Medical students formed squads and went to Bengal during their vacations to fight the epidemic.

Young people set up relief kitchens and milk canteens, distributed quinine, and approached chemists for free supplies of medicine.

They attacked hoarders' dens to get rice for Bengal.

They organized cultural squads and sports events to raise money for relief and to spread awareness on the plight of famine victims.

They donated their jewelry so that they could be auctioned to raise money for relief work.

Students in Bombay set up "Bengal corners" in colleges to present the conditions in Bengal using pictures, cartoons, and newspaper cuttings asking questions, such as "Why Bengal Starves? Where does the cash we pay, go?" and forcing the public to demand answers from the government.

Source: The above information has been sourced from journal issues from 1942 to 1946 of *The Student*, journal of the All India Student Federation, Mumbai.

During the same time, the growth of educational facilities in India saw an unprecedented increase as did the student population.[2] As a result, the number of politically aware and articulate youth rose up against the rulers, turning the nationalist struggle into a mass movement. The common goal of Independence from the British Empire gave young people a sense of purpose and ideological zeal that drew them to the movement in large numbers. As we saw earlier in Chapter 2, youth is a time of *identity formation*, and many young people in search of an identity saw the Independence movement as an *opportunity to live for their ideals*. In his oral transcript, Mr Pinto, a freedom fighter, describes

[2]In the first three decades of the twentieth century, the student population in India increased five times and the number of universities doubled. By 1936, there were 120,000 college students (Altbach 1970).

the psychological appeal of the movement on youth. "I saw thousands of people violating the various laws and undergoing self sacrifice by peacefully receiving lathi charge and imprisonment. I could not remain aloof." He had to experience what his peers and compatriots were going through. Mrs Mehra, a student in Indraprastha College in the forties, remembers the charged atmosphere in University of Delhi campus. "There was rebellion in the air. Students used to jump the wall of IP college to attend meetings." Campuses were transformed into venues for political activism with students making posters, banners and placards, distributing leaflets, and joining demonstrations and public meetings demanding freedom.

The *political leadership* also actively encouraged youth social action and was a huge influence on young people. In 1920, Gandhi called upon students to boycott schools and colleges and participate in the movement.[3] Later, in 1929, he also appealed to students to devote their holidays to village service during which they could conduct literacy classes, raise awareness on sanitation and attend to the ill. Like many other students, Mr Lal was inspired to run away from hostel to join Gandhi at Sewa Ashram, Wardha, only to be sent back and told to return after he completed his education. But besides Gandhi, there was a *galaxy of leaders that inspired confidence* and motivated young people. Bhagat Singh, Chandrashekhar Azad, Jawaharlal Nehru, Abdul Khan Gaffar, Rabindranath Tagore, and a host of others were mentioned during the interviews and in the oral transcripts. Inspired by Lal Bahadur Shastri's appeal during the Bengal Famine, Mrs Tarawati, a young bride from a village in Punjab, started keeping a fast every Monday—a habit she has continued into her eighties—so that the grain saved could be given to the poor. Not only did the leaders inspire confidence, they were also easily accessible. As a student and social secretary of the Ewing Christian College Union, Allahabad, Mr Lal recalls cycling to Anand Bhawan to invite Pandit Nehru to speak at his college. Such public appearances were common and several people we interviewed mentioned attending public meetings to hear the leaders of the Independence movement. It was also common for students to go on strike every time a leader was arrested.

Thus, we believe that the upsurge of Active Citizenship during the Independence movement was a child of its times; a river born from a

[3]This point of view saw a dramatic change after India had gained Independence when Gandhi said that students must "eschew active politics.... A student's duty is to study various problems that require solution. His time for action comes after he finishes his studies" (printed in the newspaper *Harijan*, August 7, 1947).

mountain of aspiration to be free. The *context* itself commanded the intervention of the youth (see Figure 4.7).

The movement had been growing in stature throughout the twenties and thirties but with freedom becoming imminent in the forties, it was suddenly catapulted into the main stage as *the* defining moment of the times. It became the talk of the town. Dare we say it became fashionable? Not only did it gain a societal legitimacy, freedom fighters became guests of honor at every gathering and were conferred a special status by society.

Figure 4.7: A "5th Space" during the Forties

Source: Authors.

Box 4.5: Student Action during Communal Riots, 1946

In the predominantly Hindu neighborhood of Ballygunge in Calcutta, a group of school boys aged 10–14 years wielded lathis to protect Muslim families from repeated attacks by the Hindu mobs.

Muslim students saved students from Victoria Institution for Girls, Calcutta, from being looted by a Muslim mob.

Bombay student union organized blood donation drives for riot victims.

In Bombay, students organized joint defense and peace committees for defending their localities, for allaying panic, and keeping the goonda elements in check.

After the riots, Calcutta was faced with danger of epidemics due to the neglect of sanitation. Students cleaned their neighborhoods and organized inoculation drives against diseases.

Source: Compiled by the authors.

Added to this recognition by society, there were lots of individual opportunities for learning, achievement, and a cause to boot. You could participate in the millions of interventions designed by guides like Gandhi or you could make up the rules for your own experiment, if you so fancied. There were minimal established ideologies that you had to conform to; lots of the rules of the game were emergent and based on the experiences of young people themselves. And you could act independently or in groups and still be a part of a larger change that was sweeping the country. At one level, you added to the momentum and at another you could flow along with it.

Youth clubs of West Bengal, *akhadas* of North India, *takli mandals*, *charkha* groups, student unions, political study groups, and party youth wings among others, were enclaves cocreated by young people beyond the family, career, friends, and leisure spaces that had traditionally been young people's domain.

One of the main reasons that enabled a high rate of student participation was the broad-based and inclusive nature of the movement. Everyone was welcome and contributed to the best of their capacity. There were innumerable activities that young people undertook depending on their circumstances and abilities. Some ran swadeshi stores promoting Indian products and encouraging the boycott of foreign goods, others organized strikes or unfurled the national flag, while still others cut telephone wires, derailed goods trains and bombed government offices. Everywhere young people formed their own groups so that they could initiate action—"Everybody was a leader as he did whatever he thought fit in the best interest of the country and the movement" (Narayan Mulram Wadhwani, born in Sind in 1924). The movement made it easy for everyone to participate in their own way. You did not need to court arrest and go to prison to be a nationalist. Even a young housewife confined to her home could support the struggle by buying Indian products and spinning khadi. As Pinto points out, "In every hand one could see a *takli* with which yarn was spun" (see Box 4.6).

Student activities were not limited to the big cities alone. Instead a highly decentralized system emerged to coordinate student activities. Youth leagues, debating societies, student organizations, and student unions mushroomed in most of the educational centers in the country.[4] The All India Student Federation was set up in 1936 to "prepare students

[4]Some of these cities and towns include Jullundur, Moga, Hoshiarpur, Ludhiana, Ferozepur, Gujranwala, Rawalpindi, Sialkot, Multan, Kapurthala, Jammu, Lucknow, Cawnpore, Allahabad, Aligarh, Bareilly, Meerut, Dehradun, Khurja, Barabanki.

for citizenship in order to take their due share in the struggle for complete national freedom." Within the first two years of its establishment, it had 50,000 members. However, according to Mr R. N. Bhatnagar, who grew up in the princely state of Udaipur, the freedom movement remained very much an intellectuals' pursuit. In rural areas of Rajasthan, freedom was still an alien concept. However, even in remote areas, young people remained active by building their communities and engaging in community work, such as organizing festivals and death ceremonies, looking after the ill, and helping the aged.

Box 4.6: Myriad Ways Young People Engaged in Social Action in the Forties

- Participation in Quit India processions, hunger strikes and meetings
- Designing wall newspapers highlighting national events
- Collecting donations for the movement
- Spinning and wearing khadi
- Burning and boycotting foreign goods
- Free coaching classes for students
- Relief efforts for famines and floods
- Cutting telephone wires
- Bombing government offices
- Derailment of goods trains
- "Jail bharo" (courting arrest)
- Mass and individual satyagraha
- Unfurling the Congress flag

The media too helped to fuel and spread the nationalist fervor. Many young people, such as Mr Sundarayya and Mr J. R. Sahni, used to regularly read Gandhi's *Young India* and *Harijan* and were greatly influenced by his views. *Student*—the AISF journal was widely circulated and helped not only to raise awareness on social crises, like the Bengal Famine and communal conflicts, but also to highlight the role of students in addressing these issues and appealing to the student community to look beyond the classroom and join the efforts to overcome these challenges. Several students also started printing and distributing illegal pamphlets and newspapers as well to mobilize support for the movement (see Box 4.7).

The emergence of a collective consciousness ensured that youth participation in the freedom movement was socially sanctioned. Many parents and teachers set an example and encouraged young people to join the movement. Participants commanded respect and admiration. In fact, wearing khadi and courting arrest became the fashion!

In conclusion, there were several factors that created an environment conducive to youth participation during the Independence movement: the context of the times, the growth of an educated and articulate student population, the force of the collective conscience of the country, the emergence of decentralized student federations and unions, the inclusive membership of the movement, the wide range of opportunities for participation and experimentation, the role of the political leadership, the teachers and the media, and the recognition accorded to people joining the movement. We have tried to establish that Active Citizenship was at its peak during the Independence movement. It created what can be called the 5th Space where large numbers of young people chose to hang out.

WHAT HAPPENED TO THE OTHER SPACES DURING THE FREEDOM MOVEMENT?

In this section we illustrate how the five spaces were not only closely interconnected, but how the space for Active Citizenship impacted and supported all the others.

Education and careers

With 76 percent of the respondents in our primary research claiming that education was "important" or "very important" and over 60 percent claiming that a good career was "very important" to them (see Box 4.7), it is evident that young people living at the peak of the freedom movement, were as much concerned about their education and careers as perhaps the youth of today or any other era (see Annexure 5 for the findings of the primary research). In fact, some of the female respondents, such as Shakuntala Mehra and Kushal Garg, who had been actively engaged in social action, continued their education after Independence and became postgraduates.

Box 4.7: "Your Exams and You"

You are locked up in your world of books ... but open your window and take a look outside. A destitute Indian mother in Bengal is cowering before Japanese bombs in broad daylight. Yes, study hard. We need doctors to save Indian lives and scientists and engineers to build Indian industry. But do not forget the world around you.

Source: The Student, Bombay, February 7, 1944.

What is noteworthy and different is that political engagement and social action were seen by the youth as the arena for a "real education." One could say that engagement with the 5th Space created by the freedom movement opened up young people's minds and forced them to question the existing educational system and the very purpose of education. Mrs Mehra pointed out the futility of studying when one was not free. As a student under the British Raj, it was Independence—and not exams—that was her first priority. After Independence, however, she defied her father and insisted on completing her postgraduation before getting married—illustrating how much she valued an education (Mrs Mehra, personal interview, July 9, 2010). Mr Sundarayya also questions the value of education in British India: "If ultimately all our education is just to satisfy the ruling power ... I am not bothered about such education." Instead he saw greater educational value in social action and decided to "plunge into the work" of the freedom movement.[5] Classrooms were seen as irrelevant as they "only provide instructions in different subjects" and "merely enable students to appear in university exams" (Prabodh Chandra), in contrast to jails which became the new "schools for political awareness" (Pinto). Student members of the movement were more aware of their rights and duties and conscious of the environment around them.

Young people were also influenced by teachers and professors, especially students attending national schools and colleges. The Sir Ganga Ram School in Lahore was Mrs Kushal Garg's window to the freedom movement. The principal, Mrinalini Chattopadhyay, was a staunch nationalist who inspired her students to participate in the struggle for freedom. Mrs Garg mentioned several activities aimed at building political awareness among the student community and

[5]Oral transcript, Oral History Department, Nehru Memorial Museum and Library (NMML), New Delhi.

providing opportunities so that they could participate, such as study circles, distribution of flyers against British injustice, wall newspapers, plays and cultural events to raise funds for famine and flood relief. Many of these students continued to be active even after graduating from college and getting married (Mrs Kushal Garg, personal interview, dated August 10, 2010). Mrs Kamla Rai described her years at the university in Santiniketan as a turning point in her life where she was greatly influenced by Mahatma Gandhi and Gurudev Rabindranath Tagore and embraced the national movement (Mrs Kamla Rai, personal interview, September 12, 2010). Another respondent, Mr Lal (a journalist) recalls a *prabhat pheri* demanding freedom in Meerut in which every school participated. He also mentioned his teacher—an American missionary—who motivated him to start night literacy classes for the hostel staff and to mobilize donations for flood relief (Mr Lal, personal interview, 21 August, 2010). Realizing the educational value of social action, these teachers opened their institutions to include the world, enabling students to look beyond and connect with what was going on around them. Active Citizenship and education became joined at the hip.

Family

Almost 80 percent of the respondents interviewed said that their families (parents, older siblings, grandparents, and husbands) influenced their lives to a great extent. Some young people took their cue from their parents who were staunch nationalists and active in the movement themselves. Mrs Mehra recalls her father as the first resident in Chandni Chowk, Delhi, who boycotted and burnt all his foreign goods in public, setting an example for the neighbors to follow. While parents in the employment of the British government may have prohibited their children from participating in the freedom movement, they secretly sympathized with the nationalist movement and often turned a blind eye to their children's nationalist activities, even though this could have jeopardized their livelihoods. Mr Lal recollects his father, an engineer with the Public Works Department (PWD), giving him a banned book on British atrocities and taking him to a public meeting to hear Subhash Chandra Bose. And even if parents did not turn a blind eye, as Mrs Mehra observed, the mood of rebellion was infectious and spilled into the home. So, when Mrs Garg's father, a civil engineer with the government told her he would lose his job due to her political activities, she was not deterred and continued with her political work. Similarly when Mrs Kamla Rai and her friends were arrested for organizing a demonstration in Karachi, she refused to face the "shame" of being bailed out by her father, preferring to turn him away and spend six weeks in jail.

Thus, the context of the freedom movement was generally such that the family encouraged Active Citizenship and was willing to make sacrifices if needed to participate or allow participation in the movement.

Friends

Friends played a reasonably important role in the lives of young people in the forties. Seventy-three percent of the respondents said they used to go out with friends often, and 46 percent of them claimed that their friends had influenced them. Friends were often the source of information about political activities and played a role in motivating others to join in the movement. In families that were very strict and forbade participation in the freedom movement, young people, like Mr Chatterji, used to rely on their older, more politically active friends to keep them informed.

Some very interesting data showed up on whether the youth of the forties crossed the borders of their own caste, religion, or gender while establishing friendships. As many as 86 percent of the respondents shared that they had friends from other religions. Schools (especially Christian schools), colleges, and hostels were spaces where young people from different religions could mix freely. Mr Om Prakash from the Class of 1945 in The Doon School, Dehradun, recalls losing many Muslim school friends to Pakistan after the Partition of India. However, in some cases, Muslim friends were not welcome in Hindu homes and if they did come, their dishes were kept separate leading to some awkwardness. Sixty-six percent respondents claimed they had friends from other castes with several of the educated, urban respondents claiming that they were not aware of caste. Yet it must be clarified that untouchability was frequently cited as a practice and that friends across castes were often from subcastes rather than from the so-called "lower" castes. Moreover, while marriage was an important institution for 65 percent of the respondents, only four respondents said they could marry someone outside their community (and only two actually did). One respondent referred to the practice of strict pollution rules at home and recalls bathing if he touched a Harijan by mistake. So while borders were crossed, these crossings were still within clearly defined limits.

But when it comes to friends across the gender divide, the situation was even more extreme. Only 33 percent of respondents had friends of the opposite sex. According to Mr Bhatnagar, there were few girls in the public sphere. Mrs Mahapatra who grew up in Mayurbhanj, Odisha, recollects going out in purdah. The situation was exacerbated by single sex schools and colleges and few opportunities to meet, leave alone develop a friendship. Mrs Bimla Sharma, who grew up in Mathura was sent to a boys' school because there were no schools for girls in Mathura, was made to spend the recess in the principal's office so that she was "safe" from the boys. When she reached 8th grade, the principal requested her father to take her away, since she could not be held responsible for her any longer. However, compared to the smaller towns, the environment in cities, such as Delhi, Mumbai, and Lahore was much more liberal and there was greater interaction between men and women, especially among college students. In spite of this, only two respondents chose their own partners instead of going in for an arranged marriage. In both cases, the partners belonged to a different community.

Here too, we found the space to be in the shadow of the movement as many friendships emanated from the freedom struggle and in some cases grew to encompass it.

Leisure and lifestyle

In the absence of TV and the Internet, the youth of the forties spent their leisure time in a variety of activities, such as sports, reading, and going out with friends to the movies. However, there were also organizations such as the Indian People's Theatre Association (IPTA) that raised awareness on social issues, such as widow remarriage and other contemporary concerns, using different popular media, such as songs, dance, and theater. Mrs Mehra, a member of IPTA's Delhi chapter, recollects skipping classes to attend IPTA meetings and also participated in plays to collect money for the Bengal Famine. Contemporary art also contributed to the nationalist mood with young artists like K. A. Abbas making socially relevant films and Ali Sardar Jafri writing antiwar poems. The progressive writers' and artists' groups reflected the mood of rebellion by abandoning conventional forms of art and experimenting with new forms and subjects. Mainstream movies influenced many urban youth in the forties, who started to copy the fashions they saw on screen. Apart from fashions, movies such as *Achut Kanya* took up socially relevant themes, for example, inter-caste marriages, and influenced young people's attitudes toward these themes. Coffee houses were meeting grounds for college students and venues for animated discussions on politics and the struggle for emancipation. The movement was the place to be in, and students who could not participate in these circles were almost pitied by the more active students.

As discussed in this section, the freedom movement captured the imagination of the Indian society and encompassed all the other spaces in a young person's life, including family, studies and careers, friends, and leisure. For many young people in the forties, like Mrs Kushal Garg, Mr Lal, and Mrs Rai, the movement took over every aspect of their lives. However, it was not at the expense of the other spaces. Participation in the freedom movement did not necessarily mean stealing time and resources away from the other spaces. Instead, they coexisted and complemented each other.

WHAT HAPPENED TO THIS GREAT RIVER OF ACTIVE CITIZENSHIP?

Alas, after Independence, the adults, as argued in Chapter 2, usurped the task of building a new India. Youth were encouraged to leave governance to the adults. In politics, government, and civil society, young people were yanked off the wheel of the ship and were expected to concentrate on their studies in preparation for adulthood. They were also expected to volunteer their spare time to the ship's boiler room (as volunteers, not owners of the space) while waiting for their turn to gain the helm of affairs. As preparation for an adult future began to occupy center stage again, the upsurge of Active Citizenship dwindled back down to a duty to be performed as a citizen of the country; young people were told to "put your drop in the ocean." Consequently, Active Citizenship turned from a hangout to a "hang it" space within a couple of decades after Independence. You had to sacrifice time, effort, and energy from the other four spaces and devote it to citizenship. Slowly it was no longer sanctioned or promoted actively by society and, in many cases, actually downplayed or outright denied to young people. Ever since, citizenship has only turned more and more passive (except for a blip or two).

Did a context like the Independence movement arise again, a context that was compelling enough for young people to pour into the Active Citizenship space? There was a surge of youth involvement post Independence, around the sixties and seventies. The sixties witnessed a global outcry of youth voices in both the developed and developing countries. The reasons, however, were different in the developed countries. Mukul Manglik (Associate Professor of History at Ramjas College who has consistently worked with young people to build their perspectives and provide opportunities for social action) puts it as "everything to live with, nothing to live for" thinking in the West that led to the "rebellion" (personal interview, September 8, 2009).

In India, on the other hand, youth were frustrated with the establishment as the Nehruvian model of development was not producing results in terms of higher living standards. The economy failed to generate adequate employment. Prices were on the rise. With huge disparities, social justice was perceived as a mirage. Bureaucratic planning and implementation failed to involve young people in the nation-building process. The education system was perceived as irrelevant with high rates of enrolments but poor facilities. There was rampant corruption and nepotism in public life.

Consequently, the sixties and seventies were witness to some major movements that emerged as a response to this context. The most iconic of these were the Naxalite movement and the socialist movement led by Jai Prakash Narain. The seventies also saw the emergence of a strong NGO sector. Together, these movements drew in a large number of young people and were largely sustained by the youth of those times. Though nowhere near the upsurge of the forties, the JP movement mobilized large numbers of middle-class youth against the issues of corruption, inefficiency, ineffectiveness of the education system, the caste system, poverty, and a repressive government. Bhawanand Bhai, Ranjan Bhai, and Sitanshu Dirghangi, three activists of the era, explain that it was the charismatic leadership of JP besides the corruption and nepotism-laden context of the country which motivated a large number of young people to join the JP movement. These young people took the extreme step of quitting colleges, jobs, burning their degrees, and participated in several rallies, *morchas*, village visits to sensitize people, and also spent time in jail. Chinnapan, an NGO leader in Villupuram in Tamil Nadu, explained how one of the significant catalysts for orienting young people toward Active Citizenship, especially in Tamil Nadu, was the social context of the times, for example, the Dravidian movement and the Dalit rights struggle. Bodies such as All India Catholic Universities Federation (AICUF) stirred Chinappan and scores of other young people to engage in social action.

The context of the times was, therefore, that of a failure to deliver on the promises of the freedom movement, and perhaps the frustration was a result of unmet expectation—that Independence will usher in a more just society.

In Chapter 2, we spoke of the murmurings of a revival of Active Citizenship in the second half of the first decade of the new millennium, thanks to a contextual interest being generated by the global collapse of systemic, political, and economic ideologies coupled with the Climate Change crisis, all of which streamed into homes by a proliferation of new and old media-propelled visuals of the image revolution. It has indeed become somewhat of a trend of inverted snobbery, especially among a small section of urban middle-class youth, to become a "Global Active Citizen," though it's nowhere close to a mainstream idea as yet.

The CSDS survey (De Souza, Kumar, and Shastri 2009) acknowledges the Active Citizenship space among youth today by locating three of their seven rubrics (namely Politics and Democracy, Governance and Development, Nation and the World) firmly in it. The results of the survey in these rubrics confirm that Active Citizenship has been relegated to the fringes of the mind space of youth in contemporary India. Two-thirds of the young people surveyed show little or no interest in politics. Only 20 percent of the respondents said they have participated in protests, rallies, and demonstrations. In contrast, more than 70 percent of the respondents show a strong to moderate belief in democracy. Some commentators might cite the voting turnout among young people as a clear sign of youth interest in politics. In fact, the CSDS report vouches for this view by reporting that 47 percent of the young people surveyed had voted in all or major elections since they came of voting age. Like we said, many discourses, especially the market-oriented ones, would commend this finding as an endorsement of democracy but in our perspective, reducing citizenship to voting would be displaying the tendency to approach an ocean with a spoon.

Aristotle has described a citizen as "someone who participates in political affairs" (Arthur and Davies 2009) and Pericles adds: "Just because you don't take interest in politics doesn't mean politics won't take interest in you." By participation in political affairs, Aristotle does not mean voting alone. Rather, he explains it as taking time out from the career to discuss affairs of the state.

Young people in India today seem too preoccupied to heed Aristotle and Pericles; careers are at the center stage of their life experience. It's true a large number of young people attended the rallies against corruption in India in August 2011 and though there is a context of rising prices and frustration with politicians, it is in the shadow of the great corporate juggernaut that rolls on relentlessly. With the India growth story intact, we believe, a young person's political vision too will remain obscured by the clouds of hopes of a good career with a high earning potential. Living is what happens while you are earning a living. To draw young people away from this pot of honey will require upping the ante through brinkmanship games played out like a reality show on the electronic media. But it will not be easy to whip up crowds in the same way every time as it happened during Anna Hazare's hunger fast of August 2011, without the backing immediacy of a starkly deteriorating context in the country.

We would be like ostriches with our cynical heads buried in the sand, if we were to claim that the country is going through dire straits. If we view ourselves on economic indices alone (keeping aside the social indices) we seem to be doing pretty well. In fact, many would argue that we are on the ascendant like never before; all figures in the financial and economic world, urban infrastructure, sport, or cultural spheres are on the rise. In fact, it is being claimed that amidst the global decline, India is well placed to become a superpower "if only our political class would wake up to the opportunity." We are living in times that cannot remotely be compared to the context that prevailed during the forties or in the seventies. We repeat: a river is born from a mountain of aspirations. And today's youth aspire, above all else, to get a piece of the growing gross domestic product (GDP) cake of our country.

If there is a section of youth who are ready to explode, it's the marginalized sections in both rural and urban realms. The most worrying thing in this country today is not corruption; it's the unequal distribution of the cake. As the poor—unemployed and unemployable—wait for the crumbs to trickle down, their anger is being stoked by all kinds of civil society and political combines. The context of these huge inequalities could provide the reality and immediacy for an uprising but that won't be anything like the peaceful, Gandhian, largely middle-class urban one witnessed at the Ram Lila grounds in August 2011.

Another worrying trend of recent times concerning the Active Citizenship space needs to be reiterated. Active Citizenship is in danger of being reduced to "volunteering" in an adult-led space, typically an issue-based NGO or movement. Most programming in the development sector today tends to be in this format. The government through its NSS and NYKS initiatives and the NGOs with their invitation to join a myriad of issue-based causes urge young people to do their bit for society by volunteering their time. Most development sector architects look at youth as *instruments of social change.* Constructed like this, this space is just like other spaces: adult-governed, beset with heavy and long-entrenched problems and boring to boot. Performing a duty—however beautifully it is dolled up and sold—can hardly be an exciting space that will pull in large numbers of young people.

The middle class feels that common spaces and social issues are the government's or NGO's business; this class of society wants its children to keep their noses clean and ready for sniffing out job opportunities wherever they can. Of course, if the college in the USA values community service, then parents encourage their children to spend time volunteering because "it's important for your admission into college to get the right recommendations and certificates."

We believe that the twin reasons of *(a)* reduction of Active Citizenship to volunteer for social change and *(b)* being out of tune with the aspirations of the times will never allow Active Citizenship to gain mainstream societal legitimacy, at least not in the next decade or two. Constructed as Active Citizenship currently is, it will remain a fringe activity for a handful of alternative youth with some aberrant blips here and there.

HOW DO WE REIMAGINE ACTIVE CITIZENSHIP TODAY SUCH THAT IT CAPTURES THE IMAGINATION OF THE MAINSTREAM?

At the moment the five spaces relate to each other somewhat, as illustrated in Figure 4.8.

Figure 4.8: The 5th Space Today ... in the Margins

Source: Authors.

Career and career-related studies are at the center, a much larger circle than all the others depicting the lion's share it claims of young people's time, effort, and other resources. The Active Citizenship space, as we said earlier, plays a marginal role among mainstream youth, being largely populated by some die-hard young people who volunteer part of their time toward issues they are passionate about.

We believe the Active Citizenship space needs reimagining to increase its attraction for mainstream youth and to gain societal sanction. We will let Aristotle guide us in this landscaping reshuffle. Consider his proclamation: "To be a good human being you have to be an active citizen but it need not be true the other way round." Which means you could be a good active citizen but not a good human being. It's not difficult to think of strident activists who are undemocratic, conniving, and self-absorbed with their own goals. That is where we believe, the nub of the problem lies.

Our latest experiments at Pravah with reimagining the 5th Space had begun to focus strongly on Aristotle's words (though we have come upon them only recently). We believe the 5th Space must focus as much on the *self-transformation* of young people as it does on transforming society through them. We have reconstructed the 5th Space to reinforce this identity-formation stage of youth; "it's the time of a million first impressions" is the learning we took away from the developmental theory of youthhood described in an earlier chapter. Good human beings, and not only good active citizens, are the desired results of our experiments.

The processes of learning in this 5th Space flow from Self to Society, from Me to We, rather than the other way round. *Recognizing the oneness between the inner and outer worlds of young people is the key.* While impacting society, young people impact themselves and if facilitated properly these experiences will lead to heightened consciousness of the Self and the ego, enhanced leadership skills (like problem solving, decision-making, team working, conflict positive, dialoging, etc.), relationship-building capabilities, and value and knowledge-based stances on social issues. These three together—the Self, relationships, and Society—we believe, stretch the current definition of Active Citizenship which focuses only on social issues. Thus, in our reconstruction of the 5th Space, Active Citizenship (defined today as volunteering in NGOs and government development sector), is only one drop in the colorful ocean of the 5th Space. We have declined to give this space a name (like Active Citizenship) because we believe the real owners/parents of any space reserve the rights for its christening.

Leaving the further detailing of our experimentation with the 5th Space to a separate chapter, let's describe this space loosely as of now, as a co-created transforming experience for young people. To repeat, it includes developing the Self, relationships, and engagement with society. Denizens of this 5th Space, as Aristotle said, work first and foremost at becoming better human beings.

Using this wider definition of the 5th Space, let's also consider its positioning vis-à-vis the other four spaces now (see Figure 4.9). Conceptualized thus, the 5th Space is not a tiny island separated from the others by a sea of sacrifice impossible for most to cross; in effect, it is a space that strengthens the other four and could even encompass all the others. It is central in helping the young person to choose and lead a more effective career, become a more supportive and understanding family member, a trustworthy friend, and a conscious and responsible maker of leisure and lifestyle choices. Indeed it is the 5th Space that makes the other four count too.

For those skeptics who might have reservations in putting the 5th Space at the center stage of spaces occupied by youth, as we are advocating,

Figure 4.9: The 5th Space: Making the Other Four Count Too

Source: Authors.

we have the following questions. Our question to a corporate/government/ NGO recruiter would be: "Wouldn't your organization be best served by a young person who has developed a good EQ, a sorted out value system, great leadership abilities and a mature worldview?"

Our question to parents would be along similar lines: "Would you like your ward to be able to stand on his/her own feet confidently, know how to live rather than just earn a living, and to handle conflicts positively along the way?" To friends we would like to ask: "Wouldn't you want to hang out with a person who keeps his/her commitments, is a sensitive listener, empathizes with you and doesn't judge you too quickly?"

If you agree that this is the kind of young person society and the other spaces would be best served by, then join us in rearranging the landscape such that the 5th Space occupies its rightful prominence.

For the idea of the 5th Space to grab center stage, we need to reposition it as the nurturer of all the other spaces. To accomplish this, how should the 5th Space be designed? How would it be different, yet supporting the other spaces? How can it include more than just Active Citizenship in its agenda? How can it make the other four count?

In the next chapter we talk of some of the ways in which we can bring the 5th Space to the center of the youth development discourse. But before we go there, let's see what we can learn from a 5th Space that became a high priority for mainstream youth.

To end this chapter, let's summarize the key learnings that emerged from our study of the Independence movement in creating a widespread but deep, vibrant, and sustained engagement of youth.

1. The Independence movement in the forties was a legitimate space for young people in the eyes of the family, teachers, and society in general. Considering that the family continues to be a source of huge support for young people as evinced in the CSDS study, we need to *legitimize our current 5th Space formulations for family acceptance*, like the freedom movement had been able to do. We not only have to capture the imagination of the young people but also their parents and other influencers.
2. Not only was it legitimate, the freedom movement was also the chosen place to be in. Students who did not participate in the 5th Space were pitied since the perception was that they were missing out on all the fun and action. Participation was not a duty and definitely not a chore. In fact, this space spilled into and impacted the other four spaces. While there were structures in place to coordinate different efforts, young people had the freedom to

self-organize and start their own initiatives to further the movement. Everybody was a leader and did what he or she thought would help. Therefore the 5th Space of today needs to develop *a culture that welcomes and allows young people to self organize, design, and take ownership for the space.*

3. The movement created more "border crossings" than the youth experience today, at least across the religious divide. The situation today has altered dramatically. The resultant ghettoization and conflict between caste, gender, and religion that are carried forward into adulthood are plain to see. Young people are easily brainwashed and used as instruments of terror against the "other" community who are demonized in their minds because they know no better. These are critical downstream effects of lack of opportunities to really know the "other" during adolescence and early youth. *Therefore, any 5th Space formulation must ensure plenty of such border crossings and deeper interactions between communities.*
4. Another important aspect that emerges is that students pursuing higher education were drawn to the movement in comparison with the illiterate. Therefore, our 5th Space needs to *synergize with higher education institutes.* Maybe we could tie the 5th Space into the curricula of vocational training institutes who are already mobilizing and attracting young people in large hordes.
5. We also found that the movement was able to capture every citizen's mind and heart without expecting major diversion and sacrifice of their time and energy from the other spaces. As we said earlier, there were no caste hierarchies within the freedom fighters; wearing khadi was as much a statement as going on a hunger strike or courting arrest. Without demanding sacrifice, the leaders of the movement were able to inspire by their own actions many young minds and hearts to join them. Unfortunately, the leaders of today don't seem to have that pull and at the same time there is exclusivity in entry in to the 5th Space with candle light vigils and mere voting in elections deemed as "tokenism." It is necessary to make membership of the 5th Space as inclusive as possible by creating a wide range of opportunities so that young people, regardless of their circumstances and background, can participate in ways that are practical and convenient for them.
6. As we saw, the media played an important role in influencing young people and inspiring them to join the movement. How can we use media today, especially TV, community radio, and the Internet to raise awareness and mobilize young people to join the

5th Space? To a large extent the media has contributed to youth participation in the current movements, for example, in the case of justice for Jessica Lall/Radhika Tanwar, and the anticorruption crusade. Apart from mainstream media, there are several grass-roots initiatives, such as the community video units set up by Drishti as well as Grassroots Comics (www.worldcomicsindia.com) and cybermohalla[6] that have successfully promoted citizen journalism by placing media in the hands of young people so that they can not only understand community issues but also inspire community members to address these issues.

CHAPTER HIGHLIGHTS

In summary, this chapter points toward the four spaces that have traditionally pulled in young people, that is, family, friends, careers, and leisure and lifestyle. Is there a 5th Space? Today it is limited to Active Citizenship (volunteering for a cause) and is mostly on the periphery. This Active Citizenship space has taken center stage only when there is some cataclysmic event or crisis that makes it difficult to ignore. The Independence movement was one such time; it engaged young people like never before or since and was unprecedented in the extent, depth, and longevity of participation of youth. What are the lessons we can learn from the architecture of the Independence movement? It has given us many insights in reimagining the 5th Space. But that kind of context, we believe, will never be built up again. Too many young people today are enjoying the fruits of India's growth story. So without a context, can the 5th Space be mainstreamed again? We argued that the only way this could happen would be if the 5th Space were such that it developed skills, attitudes, beliefs, and values that nurture all the other spaces. It could take center stage if we realized its fullest potential in building better human beings rather than confine it to mere Active Citizenship.

[6]Developed by Sarai, CSDS, and Ankur—Society for Alternatives in Education, the Cybermohalla (Cyber Neighbourhood) Project is a community of young practitioners who work with media forms (photography, animation, sound recordings, online discussion lists and text) to create cross-media works, texts, collages, posters, and wall magazines in media labs located in working-class areas of Delhi. Their writings and images can be seen as a rich database on the contested circumstances of life in the urban metropolis of Delhi. The Project addresses the interface between information technology and creativity in the lives of young people who live in a highly unequal society.

We conclude this chapter by reiterating that the 5th Space needs to focus as much on the self-transformation of young people as it does on transforming society through them. In the next chapter, we consolidate our insights from our study into concrete suggestions and share our experiences with other alchemists aspiring to be catalyzers of the 5th Space.

5

What Design Principles Can Help to Co-create a Vibrant 5th Space?

In the previous chapter, we developed the case for carving the 5th Space from the other four because when youth hang out in the 5th Space it makes the other four count too. Now we will conclude this book by discussing some design principles of a 5th Space that have emerged from our experiments with youth. Adults largely govern our world; young people, by choosing to occupy any of the four spaces legimitized by them (family, career and career-related education, friends, and leisure–lifestyle) agree to follow the rules that govern these spaces—-rules they haven't made, rules they haven't been consulted about, rules they cannot ask to change. Admittedly, young people haven't taken it silently; they have created islands of rebellion that have emerged out of the ocean at regular intervals. The Internet in the nineties, before the ocean swallowed it up again, was one such large tract of virtual space carved out by the young for themselves where they more or less ruled. Even now the Internet offers some safe havens for the young to hang out in, though adults look out for and usurp these "underground" spaces as soon as they gain popularity and mainstream legitimacy. Orkut and Facebook.com are the latest to be thus annexed.

Physical spaces that are governed by young people have been even fewer and far between, at least in this country, and arguably in the world. Though you can count them on your finger tips, they are a rich treasure trove for learning about the architecture of a youth-centric 5th Space beyond the spaces of family, career, friends, and lifestyle.

In the last chapter, we discovered why we need youth participation in civil society to rejuvenate the Indian Ocean and how in today's context of neoliberal, fast economic growth it will be difficult to wean young people away in large numbers from the opportunities available to further their self-interest. Times have changed drastically since the decades preceding the freedom movement.

So, in the face of lucrative job opportunities and the imminent demographic dividend, any 5th Space formulation that hopes to draw in youth in large numbers, we feel, has to service the all-round needs of a young person, not just engage him or her in social action. In this chapter, we put down the broad contours of the 5th Space. How would you recognize such a space? While claiming that we would not like to define it very conclusively, all the same, we believe it's important to frame the space in terms of broad directions and governing principles.

Through our research, we have explored in detail existing 5th Space islands at the ground level and at the same time set up and learnt from our own experiments for discovering a 5th Space that can take center stage and nourish all the other four spaces. Though we may not have reached the elusive El Dorado yet and, in fact, possibly, there is no one such formulation, these 5th Space voyages have convinced us that it is the existence and easy access of many such 5th Spaces for all sections of young people that can transform society.

This transformation will come about when young people are able to cut through the multitude of stories sloshing about in the world today (the ocean of motions as we call it) and get real about themselves and the world around them; most importantly, the youth of today need to regain their understanding of how their inner world is connected to the outer world.

Since admitting our limited success in inspiring mainstream youth to change the world, we have refocused our strategic lenses considerably. Now we look at all our programs and indeed our organization itself as a 5th Space where the Self is foregrounded as much as the Society. Like we said, we don't claim to be the master architects of a 5th Space but we do have many insights to share. At the same time, to be honest, we are still figuring what works best in this space—should it be completely youth-led or co-facilitated by "adults," for instance. And yet there is no doubt on the verdict that young people get attracted to this new formulation of the 5th Space in much larger numbers, like teenagers to a screen. In fact, the more experimental the space is, the better for them; it gives them a chance to cocreate it, rather than join an already constructed one. We would like to share credit here for the following insights with the many youngsters who have made our 5th Space voyages rich and vibrant.

Based on our experiences, we suggest some principles that can help cocreate and govern the 5th Space. We also bring out the qualities/indicators that populate the character of a young person who has engaged significantly with the 5th Space. In short, we focus our lens on how to develop Aristotle's "good human being."

WHAT'S UNIQUE ABOUT THE 5TH SPACE?

Orhan Pamuk, the Nobel Prize winner for literature, has said that any story, novel, experience, or space has a heart, a core around which everything revolves. The heart uniquely differentiates this entity from another similar thing. What's the differentiator of the 5th Space?

Is it the offer of a secular quest into the Self? Let's use this question as a torch to identify the unique contours of the 5th Space. Why give the Self so much emphasis, many activists have enquired of us. The answer is self-evident. Young people aspire to discover their identities more than anything else at this stage of their development. In the context of a growing emphasis on individuality and differentiation, the Self quest has gained an importance like never before (arguably) in all sections of society. We recognize this reality and work with it rather than lament or hope this self-absorption didn't exist. Is that one of the defining principles of the 5th Space? Start from where the energy of the young people wants to go.

Ever since the Renaissance the emphasis on the Self has grown deeper with every generation. Our firm belief that the 5th Space should be constructed around what young people want and not only what the country needs, guides us in giving the Self a very significant billing in our 5th Space experiments. Roger Shanks (1993–1994), the famous learning expert has said, "Interest is a terrible thing to waste."

Till now, the Self quest has been conducted mainly by religious and spiritual gurus to whom young people from all walks of life have flocked. Among another section of youth, Linda Goodman and other astrology-based solutions are very popular. "What's your sun sign?" is a favorite question in youth conversations, even spawning a Bollywood film by that name. So we felt, why not provide young people with a secular journey into the Self? The Constitution does not mandate it as a right but we feel that begs the question about how then are young people supposed to be guided in this journey. Doesn't the State leave a yawning gap in helping along a young person's identity quest and, thus, leave the space open for religious gurus and godmen to fill?

Let's go back to our question about what differentiates the 5th Space from other spaces. Does the uniqueness of the 5th Space, then, come from being essentially an inward bound voyage? A secular way to get to know yourself better? Our answer to this question is a firm "no." It is much more than just a quest into the Self. The current Vice Chancellor of University of Delhi, Professor Dinesh Singh, puts it well. He says, "All real learning is ultimately about the Self, including subjects like Maths (which he teaches). If you can't relate Maths to yourself, then you haven't learnt it at all." Extending this philosophy to social issues, we argue that it is in grappling with these issues that young people learn even more about themselves than they do about the issue itself. If we can process the experience outside connecting it to the inner Self of a young person, tracing its impact on their impressionable identity, we believe their learning about social issues becomes real.

We start with their interest in themselves and gradually shift their gaze outward to learn about the world and social issues—inside out. As they are at the age where first impressions are lasting, we figured if we help them at this critical point to get the "right" kind of experiences early on and facilitate deep reflections vis-à-vis these real-world experiences, then we could become key contributors to the deep wiring that is going on inside them. By letting the real world seep into them consciously, we believe, they learn about the world as well as themselves.

At the same time, while facilitating this indulgence with the Self, we are acutely aware and concerned not to let this quest turn into a kind of self-absorption. At the appropriate time, the gaze has to shift back on to Society. And that timing is of grave importance, we have realized.

By acting on social issues they are passionate about, young people develop relationship and leadership skills, learn about meta-processes like how their value ranking affects their stances, how systems thinking is better than linear thinking, how to learn better, how to continuously build self-awareness and deep empathy. They realign their inner elements to their real purpose that they discover and articulate during this journey.

It is this entire voyage from Self to Society and back that together forms the heart of the experience of the 5th Space. In impacting society, young people impact themselves. This is best exemplified in a quote attributed to the Buddha: "The foot feels the foot when it hits the ground." The 5th Space allows young people to learn more about themselves by relating to society and impacting it positively. In our experience, we have found that in the bid to transform the world, young people at the same time transform themselves.

The story of one of the students from the Indian Institute of Technology (IIT), Delhi, who joined the Pravah SMILE (Students Mobilisation Initiative for Learning through Exposure) program (see Box 5.1), illustrates this journey from Self to Society and back. As T. S. Eliot (1962, p. 145) has said,

Box 5.1: The Making of a "Human" Engineer

As a first year IIT student, Harsh belongs to privileged elite already slated for "success." He will graduate and become a civil engineer with the potential to influence many lives. Till then, however, the intense competition between students will ensure that Harsh and his classmates have little time for anything else other than their books, exams, and rankings. So it was a surprise to hear that Harsh had applied to Pravah's SMILE internship program[1] to go on an exposure visit to Narmada Bachao Andolan. It seemed to be a fun thing to do during the summer holidays instead of just hanging out at home!

Before leaving for the exposure visit, Harsh was convinced that *big dams are necessary for national development. There is no alternative. Of course, some villagers will be displaced in the process but then this is a small price to pay. Someone has to sacrifice for the larger good*. He was not open to any other perspectives.

The exposure visit is designed as a process with preparation through workshops on the Self and orientation to social issues. The experience gives students an intimate feel of life in a village and includes structured yet flexible spaces for self-reflection and learning during the journey as well as at the end. Harsh lived with the villagers, visited several affected villages and the dam site. He also had many opportunities to interact with project-affected people, government officials as well as activists involved with the movement. Seeing the situation first hand, he gradually became aware of a different reality. This is what he and his friends said about their experience[2]:

> Sitting with the fishermen at Dharaji, huddled around a lantern, I slowly started seeing things differently. They were living on the edge

We shall not cease from exploration
And the end of all our exploring
Will be to arrive where we started
And know the place for the first time.

We end up where we started but we look at the starting place very differently now. The reason is because we suddenly understand how we are connected *to* it. The trick that can yet save this planet, we believe, is in helping the young person to own up to the *to* in the journey from Self to Society.

---

[1]See www.youtube/5th space.com.

[2]This is based on an interview (dated February 8, 2010) with IIT students who went on a group exposure to Narmada Bachao Andolan in December 2009.

of a cliff. Before the dam, they could fish freely and there was plenty available. Now, there was hardly any fish and what's more, they needed a license to fish. Many had lost their means of livelihood and become daily wage laborers. The shadow of despair loomed large on their faces. I felt their loss and sorrow. My strong emotions took me by surprise.

Gradually, Harsh's deep empathy for the villagers gave way to questioning.

Till now I had only heard of the advantages of dams—irrigation, no floods, industries, electricity ... but the indirect fallout are rarely reported. What about the fertile land that has been submerged? People who have been displaced and lost their livelihoods? Shouldn't the social and environmental impact also be considered? Who is accountable for this loss and suffering?

Sharing his experiences with the other students in the group, Harsh was able to look inward and reflect on his own attitudes and stereotypes.

At the orientation camp, I remember thinking what will I learn from these villagers who are not even literate. But when I started listening to Sarita di and the others, I began questioning my definition of literacy. They had a deep understanding of their surroundings and explained with passion and eloquence how different, seemingly discrete aspects were, in fact, connected with each other—from the dam, to Bt Cotton, to climate change ... I wondered how she knew so much and realized that their lives were being torn asunder because of what I had till now called development.

In search of answers, Harsh began to confront himself:

We keep blaming the system. But who is the system? For a change I do not have any answers! Instead I have to look in the mirror and ask myself some hard questions: Am I ready to give up my city comforts of an air conditioner and electricity? Yesterday I did not want people to be displaced, but today I want my air conditioner. Yes, *we* are the ones who keep changing our stances.

The visit helped him to come face to face with his true self. Claiming responsibility and ownership for the situation empowered Harsh to look for solutions:

> Why can't we look at alternatives? For example, small dams are more functional and cost effective. Did you know that 45 percent of China's energy comes from small dams?

His take-way? "Confusion!" But in the midst of this confusion, there is an immense learning. There is a need to change the stories he has told himself or bought into till now. He is forced to Get Real.

> I have realized that all development has a human angle. It is not just about statistics but about human faces—faces with names, feelings, sorrows, and joys. Our role as engineers is not just to build dams, but to change life for the better. I don't just want to be just another engineer ... I want to become a more human engineer.

After he graduates, we hope Harsh remembers his promise to himself. If he does, we have a promise to make too. Pravah's Change Looms program pledges support for him to start (through seed incubation and mentoring) a project on creating small dams in the hinterland. His internships and volunteering experiences during college would have given him an opportunity to develop the skills and attitudes to lead such a social entrepreneurship project successfully by helping him to explore his Self, his relationships, and to take ownership for common spaces.

Having glimpsed what lies at the heart of the 5th Space experience, let's look at how to construct such a space. By focusing on the space rather than on individuals, we keep our eyes on the soil, not wasting too much of our time worrying about the plant itself. We already know that what we sow we reap, but here we are asking you to pay attention to what we *sow in* because it is as, if not more, important as the seed. For it will outlive this crop and nourish plants for many seasons to come.

WHAT ARE THE KEY PRINCIPLES THAT COULD SHAPE THE ARCHITECTURE OF A 5TH SPACE?

As we argued before, while referring to Active Citizenship, the actual renaming and defining of a 5th Space should, in fact, be left to young people themselves. We believe 5th Spaces are not an exclusive domain to be constructed by development sector organizations for their target groups; in fact, they could be co-created within any institution that wants to attract and build a community of young people. This could (rather, as we agreed in an earlier chapter, it should) include issue-focused NGOs, a government youth program like NSS and NYKS, orphanages, *balwadi*s, *anganwadi*s, schools and colleges, vocational training centers, corporate sector BPOs and banks, even the defense forces (who look to recruiting large numbers of young people), political party youth wings, religious institutions, like church youth wings, or the RSS and civil society movements like the Narmada Bachao Andolan and India against Corruption that draw from the energy of the young.

Outside of structured institutions too, 5th Spaces could flourish in families, friends circles, in neighborhoods and *basti*s (slums), or in youth clubs including sports groups.

Rather than defining what a 5th Space should be, we feel each 5th Space should have its own look and feel, a unique stamp given by its co-creators. Yet the outcome would be common (Aristotles' good human being) and so would the principles that govern the processes of a 5th Space. We would like to outline some of these that have proved immensely useful in our experiments with the 5th Space. These are listed in the spirit of open architecture, that is, the architects of a 5th Space can add, subtract, modify, and apply as they please. We hold no copyright on these principles, though we do hope that people will share credit with us as they go ahead and put their own signatures to the experiment.

Ownership is the key

We believe it is the people who inhabit a space and make meaning out of it, who are its real owners. Sure, others invest time, money, and effort too but let's call them investors or facilitators, not owners of the space. Like the corporate sector has done through the share market, we don't want to create owners without ownership—people who are outside the space, absentee landlords who only care about the output without bothering about the processes that will nurture the soil.

But psychological ownership can't be given; it has to be taken. In fact, this form of ownership seeps in slowly into the people, as and when the structures and people who govern the space and its culture allow it to. Let's list some of the ways in which the space can instill ownership in young people:

1. If we create a core group of young people to lead the space and take critical decisions regarding the space, we would be creating a

conducive structure for ownership to be taken. The same effect could be obtained by building an inclusive culture where *decision-making* is a consensual process. So we could intervene structurally or culturally to create a space where young people take more ownership by giving young people a significant say in decision-making. At Pravah, crucial operational, strategic, people, and financial decisions are taken by an Organization Review Group rather than by the board or the CEO alone.

2. Ownership also comes from putting in your own brick at the time when the building is being constructed. Being a part of the formulation always gives the founder members a sense of ownership that is difficult to dilute. Therefore, we feel it is imperative, at the time of creating a 5th Space, to hold blank paper consultations and *co-visioning* workshops with young people to set an agenda together.

   The evaluation mechanism at The YP Foundation brings together all volunteers, staff, and board members every quarter for a series of brainstorming meetings during which they develop the mission and goals of each program divison, review, and evaluate each project.

3. When newcomers enter, they may not have had a chance for co-creating but they should not feel left out. All the existing and new players of a space must have an avenue for self-expression that will give them the sense of ownership for the space. While they are allowed to express themselves freely, there should be co-established rules that protect others' rights from being infringed upon. YUVA's Maharashtra Yuva Manch is an example where young people have self organized into a semi-political grouping that allows them to express their voices freely on issues that concern them.

4. Young people feel ownership and respect for a place that helps them to learn. Designing the space such that young people become responsible for their own learning, have many opportunities for *learning together, and build each other's capabilities* has helped develop the context where young people take ownership. An example of ownership building through learning together is PUKAR where young people research issues in their own area in groups and learn in depth about their own neighborhood.

5. Finally, sharing results, rewards, and consequences emanating from actions in the 5th Space, with all the denizens, is a crucial

process that facilitates young people in taking on ownership for the space. Doosra Dashak's village-based youth forums exemplify this approach. In Pali district for example, where maternal and child health indicators were very poor, youth forum members started connecting the ANMs with the tribal communities so that tribal women and children can access health services. A recent survey shows improved health status in the district. Today, the local government contacts the youth forum whenever they want to organize a health camp. This shared outcome has in turn strengthened the members' ownership of the space.

Who's in charge of the space?

After freedom was obtained, adults took control of governance of the country, starting a decline in young people's concern for common spaces thereafter. In our experience too, we have found that unless young people themselves have a significant say in the governance of the 5th Space, they do not flourish to their fullest potential. Taking on this responsibility can be a hugely transformational experience.

Another of our experiments, Commutiny—The Youth Collective illustrates this point. It's a collaboration of youth development organizations that is a design think tank for architecting 5th Spaces. Here, we help organizations overcome 5th Space design challenges.

About three years ago, one of our programs—the Learning and Leadership Journey—that gives young people the space, resources, and guidance to set up their own grassroots social experiments, faced a near revolt from its first batch of commutineers (our term for the social entrepreneurs who were selected).

The first day of our six-day initiation workshop had the young activists up in arms. They felt we had been high-handed and not transparent enough during the selection process. And further, they didn't feel included in the way we had set up the initiation workshop without understanding their real needs.

The facilitators/board members of the collective conferred together and realized that indeed we had been too controlling of the process till now and though it had not been our intent, we were now faced with an "us versus them," "hostellers versus hostel wardens" kind of standoff.

Fortunately we were open and listening for the real source of discontent. Immediately we decided to go back to the drawing board and came up that very evening with a plan for including the commutineers more comprehensively in the meta-governance of the journey. Though they had been in charge of their own individual journey, we had missed out in building a shared leadership space for their collective voyage. In the running of the common journey, we had assumed charge.

Our plan of handing over/sharing the load with the comutineers paid great dividends. We facilitated an election of a core group from among them to govern learning, reporting and event management of the group's journey. As it progressed, the core group shared a large part of the staff hub's responsibility; thus freeing up the latter to facilitate, mentor, and nurture the young people in their journeys. The core group has since become an important feature in harnessing the true potential of collective leadership and also has been a great learning space for the young people.

As facilitators and architects of the 5th Space, we learnt from this experience that though young people loathe adult governance and scatter at the first signs of being bossed around, they do welcome light nudges in the right direction. Sometimes they are not able to take leadership due to lack of experience or even capability, or there might be a peer conflict, and an external, *unbiased* facilitator is required to break logjams in the group-formation stage. Also the facilitator helps individuals with one-on-one mentoring and counseling. Typically young people who are trained to be facilitators or other senior facilitators with an ability to connect with young people are central to this work and, therefore, the scaling of 5th Space ventures depends acutely on the continuous availability and supply of sensitive facilitators, who can walk the thin line between stirring the fish and letting it cook. They have to know when they should let things self-organize through peer conversations and when to stir it up in case young participants seem to be avoiding confrontations. Unfortunately, the wisdom to know which situation needs which kind of intervention can only come with experience; hence, the venture requires not only availability but also longevity of people to be involved with an experiment.

Young people like to go from what they know to what they don't

This is a well-appreciated learning strategy. Applying this to our work, we have found that starting with awareness of the Self and then moving to the young person's immediate neighborhood and then onward to larger social causes is usually a better route to take than immersing them straightaway into a social conflict situation without much preamble as we were doing earlier. Turning their gaze inward first gives them a confidence and an understanding of how their lives are connected to common spaces. Without the knowledge of the why, what, and how, it is only the faithful, the stupid, or the converted who can jump straight into social action—which is why our strong recommendation on building youth leadership is to go inside out.

Refl-action is the preferred vehicle for learning

Our 5th Space experiments have turned our traditional understanding of learning on its head. That is, we now believe learning starts from the feet and travels upwards to the head rather than the other way round. At Pravah, we call this process "refl-action". It is the action in the real world that gives the young person the much needed fodder for reflection and learning from mistakes. Of course, reflection must precede and succeed action. Action without thinking first is like shooting an arrow without a target. And reflection without action is to look at a target without a bow and arrow at hand. At Pravah, classroom workshops are only an initiation into a learning journey; they are never an end in themselves. The workshops always end with a refl-action plan and also, critical reflection processes, pauses, and tools are built in at this stage for the journey too. Mentoring, monitoring, and closure are based on the refl-action plan and the analysis of the progress toward key learning milestones.

Without markers, the journey can be a long and winding road to nowhere

We need to recognize this nature of the road we will encounter. Specific, measurable, and realistic milestones and goals are particularly difficult to identify. Yet, we need markers if we are not to get lost in the self indulgent labyrinth of identity seeking. Since this work, by its very nature, has elusive destinations, qualitative impact and frequent setbacks, it's best to describe *measures* for all the important elements—Self, relationships, and Society—before you set off on the voyage (see Box 5.2 and Annexure 6 for an indicative list of these measures developed through a consultative process with like-minded organizations).

Box 5.2: Developing an Impact Assessment Framework for Youth Interventions

In May 2010, Pravah and Innovations in Civic Participation organized a consultative process that brought together a diverse group of stakeholders to develop competencies and indicators for youth development. Participants identified three critical parameters around which they felt it was important to assess changes in young people:

1. *Understanding the Self:* Self-awareness, self-esteem, ability to learn, self-expression, and making lifestyle choices.
2. *Interpersonal Relationships:* The ability to develop effective relationships and manage group processes. Respect, appreciating diversity, group membership, building consensus, and collaboration.
3. *Impact on Society:* The ability to impact society: *(a)* recognize elements of a system, *(b)* design an appropriate intervention, *(c)* implement the intervention as active citizens, *(d)* evaluate the intervention.

(See Annexure 6 for a list of the indicators under each of the parameters.)

To give young people a chance to be the captains of their own voyage and track their own personal growth and development over time, Pravah (with help from a sister concern, Vyaktitva), building on these indicators derived from the consultation, has developed a multipoint reflection and feedback tool called the Vyaktitva Explorer (*vyaktitva* means character). This tool enables young people to map their stories for the different elements that make up our identity. Following this, you can also diagnose areas of potential change and self-transformation. We will return to this tool a little later in this chapter.

The 5th Space should foreground the now rather than the future

The space needs to be designed for balancing the long term with the present. Let's not forget that youth are not merely adults in the making. They have emotions, needs, desires, and aspirations emanating from their immediate context in the here and now.

Unfortunately, in a society obsessed with purpose and future, the present moment finds no place. It is unfortunate because the emotional growth of young people requires a focus on the now. Feelings like love, camaraderie, trust, and friendship require the soil of the present moment to thrive in. To help young people learn how to relate better to each other, the 5th Space needs to ensure opportunities for emotional release and connecting.

The focus on the now of the 5th Space brings the ambience of the space to the center stage. We mention a few characteristics that are critical in defining the *sifat, the character* of the 5th Space.

1. *First and foremost young people need to trust and be trusted.* Rebellion may be romantic but not everybody is born to it. We have found that if there is a safety net young people can trust, especially women, they can be persuaded to step outside their comfort zones. Youthhood is a time for testing comfort zones and trying new experiences but the experiments (for most) are attempted only in non-threatening spaces, with trustworthy facilitators and peers; in such circumstances, young people may be willing and inspired to go far, far enough for new learning and transformation. Likewise, young people need to be trusted. Too often, adults are unwilling to give up control and let go. As a result, young people do not get a chance to develop their leadership skills and remain in the shadows of adult facilitators.
2. *The "hangout" element is critical* too. Hanging out is about belonging, opting in voluntarily—a place where you feel safe and are accepted for who you are. The word connotes many things but above all it speaks of self-chosen and self-propelled endeavors performed with other like-minded individuals who together choose the pace and rhythm for their interactions. The space should pull youth in. It should not be mandated, compulsory, or pushed down their throat.
3. *The space should foster cross-border friendships.* In India especially, another important element of the *sifat* of such a space is that it must address the immense diversity of its people. As evinced in the CSDS 2009 study, caste, religion, and gender are barriers that young people hardly ever cross. Almost 50 percent youth surveyed reported that they had never or hardly ever known anybody from a different gender, religion, or caste. This is a shocking piece of statistics. Is it any wonder then that when these young people grow older, they favor their own for jobs, promotions, and votes or look at their neighbor or their colleague with suspicion because

they belong to a different gender, religion, or caste. Still there is a ray of hope. We believe, most of these 50 percent have not crossed these borders only because of a lack of opportunity rather than any deeply held stereotype about the "other." So, our 5th Space can provide that opportunity of engaging in pluralism actively, where safe border crossings can be arranged to initiate half the country's youth into friendships with the "other." This, by itself, we believe, would be a noble purpose for this space.

4. Lastly, a characteristic of the space that we have found draws in young people is that it should be *fun and joyful*. It's true, different people describe fun in different ways; so let us sidestep the definition game. Instead let's talk about what is not fun. One word sums up what is not fun. Work. As soon as the 5th Space becomes heavy and feels like work young people know it and only the diehards, driven by some kind of a duty, remain in that space. This is not to imply that the young are incapable of processing serious information. Fun, we have found, is one of the most effective ways of learning because it releases feelings that are critical for real learning rather than engaging in a mere intellectual exercise.

The 5th Space should empathize and heal

The health of the 5th Space depends not only on the way the space is constructed, but also on the denizen's state of mind. Individuals, as much as they contribute to the success of the 5th Space, could also be as responsible for spoiling the ambience due to the negative energy they bring into the space.

At Pravah, we have found that all the processes and structures and values of the system can be neutralized by an inhabitant of the 5th Space who is in a low mood. The space should not only be able to sense the feelings of the individual but should be so designed that it allows other minders of the space to intervene empathize, search, confront, and co-heal.

A 5th Space should provide rights to an inhabitant as well as duties for contributing to the health of the space. All parties involved need to take 100 percent responsibility of a conflict situation and inspire others to take their 100 percent as well.

The 5th Space should have an organic renewal algorithm built into it

Like a seed that has all the genetic information needed to produce the new plant, the space should be encoded with the ability to infuse all the new people who come in with a will to take ownership and charge of the space. When the founders of the space move on, it should not flounder but reinvent itself organically in the spirit and principles of the 5th Space.

For instance, Manzil, an organization providing learning opportunities for underprivileged young people, has a music class that has already spawned five bands over the last seven years. The space started within Manzil as a peer teaching experiment. The founder, Ravi Gulati, a good singer himself, believed that you didn't have to be an expert to share what you knew. Adding to the atmosphere of trust in Manzil is the complete lack of judgment about the young person's ability. By sharing you get to know your own gaps and figure out your own growth path much better than as a mere learner. There is no *ustad* to tell you what you are doing wrong. You are expected to find your own gaps from the peer feedback you receive.

The first result of this experiment was Ekam Satyam, a common man's band, with a sound completely their own. The next year, when Ekam Satyam didn't allow entry to new members, instead of knocking on their doors again and again, Ravi encouraged the new aspirants to make their own band/building. And they did. The result was *Manzil Mystics*.

Inspired by the philosophy that they will grow when they play together, many experimental bands have since sprung up. Of these, as we mentioned, five (including Ekam Satyam) have stayed together to perform on stage. The latest organic innovation coming from the young people themselves is that the bands don't have fixed members. Musicians from a pool come together under one of the three names as per convenience, energy, and availability and then disband without holding any fixed loyalties. For example, the drummer plays in three bands. Another person is the pivot for three bands (usually new bands that succeed are anchored by an inspiring engager not necessarily the best performer).

Ravi Gulati, who earlier used to give feedback, connections, facilitate feedback and conflict resolution, has almost completely withdrawn from the space. Now, he says, he is on call. But the call never really comes. The Manzil music maker has become a self-running enterprise, so it seems, at least for now.

The format and the outputs of the 5th Space may differ in various situations but, we believe, the principles for governing the architecture of a

5th Space could be similar. In the next section we demonstrate some of these principles in action as we land on the ground to explore one of Pravah's 5th Space experiments that has been the source of major learning for us.

WHAT COULD BE A WORKING PROCESS MODEL FOR THE 5TH SPACE?

We now present an illustration of one of the experiments at Pravah in creating a 5th Space.

At Pravah we have been experimenting with the idea of the 5th Space by creating different opportunities for youth to explore themselves as they experiment with social change.

As a metaphor, we've visualized the 5th Space in the SMILE program like an hourglass (see Figure 5.1). The hourglass illustrates the flow of such a learning voyage at Pravah. It signifies the time it takes for a young person to voyage across the many zones within the 5th Space.

Open at the top, it admits many but through its narrow waist only a few pass into the lower chamber where they actually take on social action projects. Those who choose not to go forward into the second part of the hourglass due to various constraints can come back at another time. Or not. Their experience is designed to have takeaways at each stage. Each experience is significant in itself, enough to change them forever.

Once they have completed this journey, they may choose to return as facilitators of the process and embark on a new journey. Our belief in creating an open and inclusive space also means that the hour glass has many inlets and outlets. That is while the representation in Figure 5.1 is the ideal flow, young people may choose to enter the space at different points and exit as it suits them.

We would now be describing some of the key components of this journey.

Outline of a typical SMILE journey

As the *first* step in the SMILE journey, Inward Bound is an innovative way of reaching out to large numbers of students (see Figure 5.2). It invites them to embark on an exciting process of self-exploration during which they can get to know themselves better, confront, and accept their multiple identities and find ways to connect with the larger world. To ensure scale, depth, creativity, and of course quality, Inward Bound uses

Figure 5.1: The SMILE Hourglass: A Youth-centric Development Process

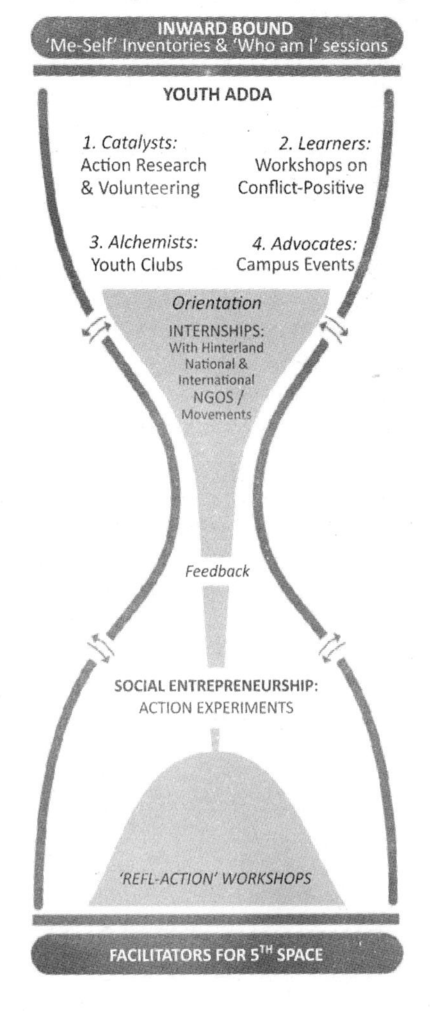

Source: Pravah.
Note: SMILE (Students Mobilization Initiative for Learning through Exposure) is a national program which was started by IGSSS and supported by Misereor. In 1995, Pravah started designing and running the Delhi Chapter of SMILE for campus youth. See www.youtube/5th spacefilm.com

myriad tools like the Myers-Briggs Type Indicator (MBTI), Identity Mapping, Leadership Inventories, simulation games like Ring Toss and Tower Building, reflective spaces like mirror walks and clay sculpting, video corners and others. All this is housed in three big attractive tents

Figure 5.2: Inward Bound

Source: Pravah.

that can be set up on different campuses so that it is easily accessible to students. The tools are simple and as self-running as possible to help young people start off on this journey. The Inward Bound tents serve as magnets to attract students and, thus, begins the journey of participation in other SMILE components. However, even if they choose not to continue, the Inward Bound experience is usually deep enough for them to learn something about themselves. Typically 100 to 150 young people experience the Inward Bound processes in the half day it is set up at a college and about 100 plus out of these typically register for further SMILE experiences. As you can see, this strategy that has no hint of social action can potentially get us a cadre of 1,500–2,000 SMILErs in a year by merely setting up 15–20 Inward Bound interventions.

Youth Adda/Youth Café

The next stage in the journey is to invite young people—both old and new volunteers—to lead and co-facilitate monthly Youth Addas (see Figure 5.3). These are common spaces created in offices, colleges, gardens, and cafés where young people meet and hang out, interact with

Figure 5.3: Youth Adda

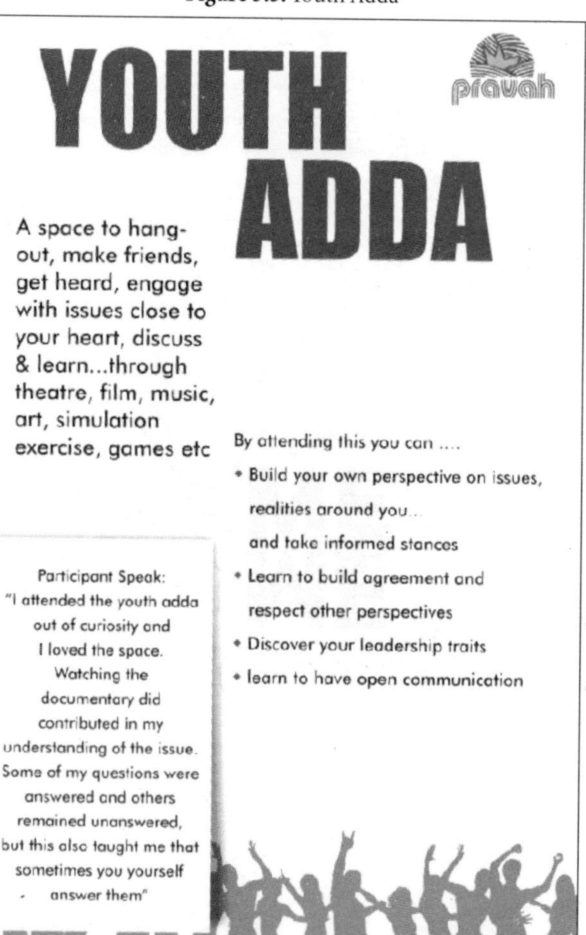

Source: Pravah.

youth of different backgrounds, have fun and organize events, workshops and exchanges to explore a theme of their own choice and learn about various opportunities to intervene and make a difference. Through this process they develop their personal and social leadership skills. Typically 30 to 50 young people attend such an Adda. The first Youth Adda after a set of Inward Bound interventions at the beginning of a new campus season typically goes deeper into the MBTI personality type indicator with a certified professional helping the young people to find out their natural preferences. Subsequently, each Youth Adda bifurcates into four possible options that the participants opt for to continue their journey. Meanwhile, the monthly Addas continue to explore themes of the young person's common choice. The youth Adda is an open program, which attracts students from different colleges and socioeconomic backgrounds. By creating memories of a shared experience over which they can bond, the Youth Adda provides young people with an opportunity to develop cross-border friendships and an appreciation for diversity.

The four options available to participants are:

1. **Catalysts:** In this option of the journey, some young participants take up social action projects in schools and colleges like action research on social issues such as communalism, cross border conflict, status of refugees, gender-based violence, environment and climate change, sustainable development. For example, in a Youth Adda last year, "In Search of My Home," a documentary film on asylum seekers in India, was screened. The 24-year-old director, Shushmit Ghosh, shared his experiences of making the film. Participants discussed the status of refugees and decided to do an action project on this issue. This was the start of Project Unnamed. Students visited the Burmese refugee settlement in Vikaspuri. They also invited an activist working with Burmese refugees to learn more about their situation. From this understanding, they developed an action plan to create awareness and help the refugees.
2. **Alchemists:** Young participants also have the option of joining youth clubs that focus on building mobilization and communication skills for social development. In the past, these clubs have used theatre, comics, and films to develop and communicate youth perspectives on a social issue. Young participants choose an issue they are interested in and go through a short training on the use of the medium. In the process of developing a product, the participants not only learn a skill and understand an issue better, they also learn to work with each other, to address conflicts, and to inspire others to support their issue.
3. **Learners:** Many participants go through formal workshops called the Conflict Positive and Get Real workshops.

Conflict Positive

This is an experience specially designed to enable young people to begin to look at conflicts in their lives positively, dig deeper, and connect their learning from conflicts they have been part of to larger social conflicts in society. They learn to position conflict as the catalyzer of change rather than merely a problem to resolve. Thus, conflicts are to be invited into a system, not avoided. We believe that conflicts between the "differences" in a system create the necessary energy for the system to self-organize from a status quo to a higher level of equality. It is only when the actors in the conflict resort to violence that the conflict becomes undesirable. Self-awareness (taking stances based on their values), leadership skills (especially consensus-building, win-win attitudes, and taking 100 percent responsibility), and knowledge about the issues are developed at this stage through practical exercises, case studies, role plays and real world application. These skills help young people to engage better in the other four spaces of career, family, friends, and leisure.

Get Real: A Deep Dive into the Self

Although Pravah has been designing from Me to We journeys for many years, there was a feeling that we focus heavily on the "We" aspect and too little on the "Me" aspect of the journey. The "to" that connects Me and We is neglected. Get Real looks at ourselves as an iceberg where the deeper elements of our personality are hidden (even to ourselves sometimes) and only the surface behaviors are accessible to us (see Figure 5.4). This is a two-to-three-day journey where we try to reach into the different defining elements of the system within ourselves.

The first question we ask is: *who are we?* We tell our participants that they are unique; just like everyone else. So instead of trying to focus on the 5 percent of our unique individuality, first we should try to understand who we are as a species. We look at human beings as the symbolic species and how the symbolic ability can be a boon as well as a bane. We discover our fears as the bane and look for boons to counter the fears and create Boon–Bane ratios that can help us be mindful of where our surface behaviors are emanating from.

We then move on to understanding the human being as Homo Narran or the storyteller. Human beings as a species are wonderful storytellers and create their world through stories. How do we learn to unravel the stories we have told ourselves and create new stories so that we can discover the Self and the world around us?

Figure 5.4: Get Real: A Deep Self-awareness Workshop

pravah

DEEP
SELF AWARENESS
WORKSHOP-GET REAL

A 2 day workshop to explore 'who am I', 'Who are WE'...and understand the deep interconnection between the two. An attempt to help you create your own story closer to your dreams

By attending this you can ....

- A deeper insight into your self and know your strengths and areas of improvement
- Recognize your passion and follow it
- Gauge, express and manage emotions
- Discover the hidden interconnections of the world
- Conflict resolution skills
- Ability to challenge your own notions and stereotypes
- Explore elements of your personality/ vyaktitva

Participant Speak:

"I have honestly looked at myself ...
it has been like the seeds and the earth after the first rain –
the scent, the fresh drops coming down and touching you.
I take back lots of strength, renewed passion, belief and support."

Source: Pravah.

How can we interpret and create authentic stories? What's the crucial role of questions in helping us accomplish this?

Right through the Get Real journey, we use a tool called Vyaktitva Explorer which we mentioned earlier (see Annexure 7). This tool helps us understand ourselves better based on facts about ourselves and true stories rather than opinions. The Explorer focuses on the five main elements that make up a human being: Sky—Purpose; Earth—Structures; Air—Values; Fire—Relationships; and Water—Meta-processes. After mapping and rating each element (using the questions given in Box 5.3), we diagnose and identify the areas of potential change and self-transformation. Finally, we look at what we need to let go and leave behind if we truly want to undertake a new journey of transformation.

Box 5.3: Exploring My Vyaktitva

Using the Explorer, Get Real helps participants to dive deep and understand themselves better. The Explorer is based on the five elements or *tatvas* of the universe, each of which symbolizes a different aspect of the character or *vyaktitva*:

Sky: To what extent is my journey influenced by my destination?

- Personal goals
- My journey toward my goals

Earth: How well do I know myself?

- Self-awareness
- Comfort with my identities
- Self-esteem and control

Air: How well-informed is my worldview?

- Value recognition
- Living the values

Fire: How deeply do I relate with others?

- Authentic relationships
- Diversity and inclusion
- Belonging
- Collaboration

Water: To what extent do meta-processes enable my journey?

- Learn-ability
- Systems thinking
- Interpreting and creating/narrating authentic stories

(See Annexure 7 for the complete version of the Explorer.)

Source: Compiled by the authors.

The feedback from participants illustrates the deep impact this process has had on them. As one of the youth facilitators pointed out: "Usually workshops are on hunger, poverty, etc. We analyze the issues but there are no opportunities to reflect on the Self. We try and change others but never turn the spotlight on ourselves."

4. **Advocates:** At this stage, young people tend to become advocates of social change and personal transformation. They take up large action projects as a collective, and lead campaigns on different themes of their choice to address the public at large and in particular their peers in schools and colleges. For several years now, SMILErs have designed and organized a youth festival called Music For Harmony. This is a space for young people to get recognition and to showcase their projects to the public, including their families and their teachers. It also helps to win support from other stakeholders and to mainstream the 5th Space in the larger world.

All of the above stages are not necessarily sequential and can happen in parallel depending on young peoples' interests, aspirations, and the context of the times. After they have gone through the Youth Adda, approximately 30–40 percent of the young participants join the next stage of the journey.

LEARNING THROUGH EXPERIENCE: EXPOSURE VISITS AND INTERNSHIPS

This part of the journey is the most intense. It requires young people to choose exposure opportunities with rural, hinterland communities and organizations or movements as well as Delhi-based NGOs. These exposure visits, volunteering opportunities, and internships enable young people to get out of their comfort zone, explore other realities, confront their own stereotypes, and understand different perspectives. In order to accommodate as many students as possible, SMILE has evolved a flexible design that offers a range of options, including short exposure visits, as well as longer internships during the holidays. These options can be located either in Delhi for those who cannot go out of the city due to family or time constraints, but typically they are with NGOs and grassroots movements working on social justice issues in different parts of the country. In addition to the individual exposures, participants can also go on a group exposure with other students. The SMILE network consists of organizations that work on a range of issues, but at the same time believes in the vision of volunteerism and can, therefore, provide valuable opportunities for volunteers. Students have been placed in organizations from Kerala to Ladakh and are working on diverse issues (see Figures 5.5, 5.6, and Box 5.4).

Figure 5.5: SMILE In-turn-ships

Source: Pravah.

Figure 5.6: Group Exposures

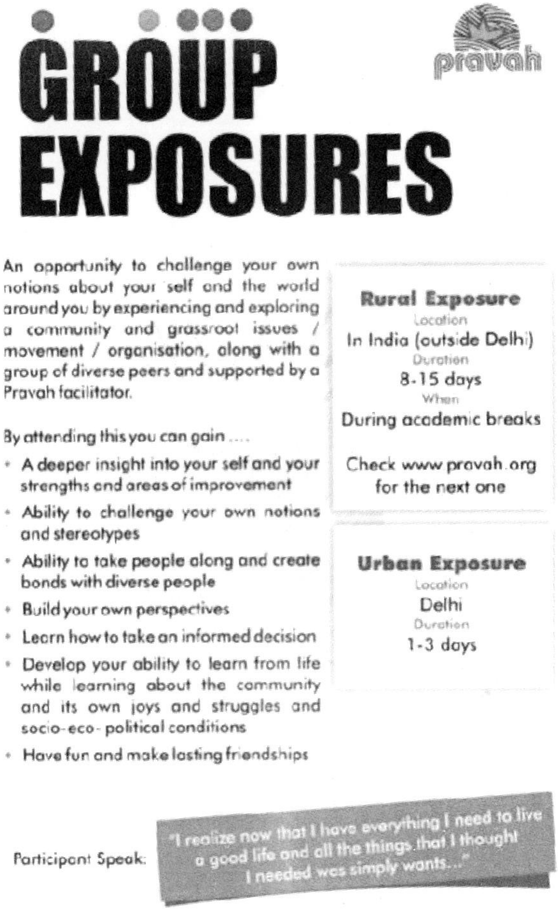

GROUP EXPOSURES

pravah

An opportunity to challenge your own notions about your self and the world around you by experiencing and exploring a community and grassroot issues / movement / organisation, along with a group of diverse peers and supported by a Pravah facilitator.

By attending this you can gain ....

- A deeper insight into your self and your strengths and areas of improvement
- Ability to challenge your own notions and stereotypes
- Ability to take people along and create bonds with diverse people
- Build your own perspectives
- Learn how to take an informed decision
- Develop your ability to learn from life while learning about the community and its own joys and struggles and socio-eco- political conditions
- Have fun and make lasting friendships

Rural Exposure
Location
In India (outside Delhi)
Duration
8-15 days
When
During academic breaks

Check www.pravah.org for the next one

Urban Exposure
Location
Delhi
Duration
1-3 days

Participant Speak: "I realize now that I have everything I need to live a good life and all the things that I thought I needed was simply wants..."

Source: Pravah.

Box 5.4: SMILE Internship Locations (2010–2011)

1. Abhivyakti, Nasik, Maharashtra
2. Drishti Media Collective, Ahemdabad, Gujarat
3. Eklavya, Bhopal, Madhya Pradesh
4. Hum Kisan Sangathan, District Jhalawar, Rajasthan
5. Jagori Grameen, District Kangra, Himachal Pradesh

6. Maharogi Seva Samiti, District Chandrapur, Maharashtra
7. Manthan, District Ajmer, Rajasthan
8. Manthan Yuva Sansthan, Ranchi, Jharkhand
9. Narmada Bachao Andolan, Khandwa, Madhya Pradesh
10. Patang, Sambalpur, Odisha
11. Sabuj Sangha, Nandkumarpur, West Bengal
12. Sampari Hukumu Bodol, Agartala
13. SBMA (Sri Bhuvneshwari Mahila Ashram), Tehri Garhwal, Uttarakhand
14. SIDH (Society for Integrated Development of Himalayas), Dehradun, Uttarakhand
15. The ANT (Action Northeast Trust), Assam
16. The Shoshit Seva Sangh (SSS), Patna, Bihar
17. Vayali, Thrissur, Kerala
18. Vishakha, Jaipur, Rajasthan

This exposure is facilitated and each of the participants has a well-designed orientation and feedback process to ensure effective refl-action. Participants attend a residential orientation camp before the visit/internship so that they can be open and prepared for the experience. Afterward, they attend a residential feedback camp that helps participants to reconnect, reflect, and share their experiences, learn from each other and bring a closure. It also helps them to explore how they can make this experience an intrinsic part of their lives (see Figure 5.7). It is a time when the group can demonstrate their commitment to the cause and design and implement an action project that addresses a social issue.

Action projects and youth facilitators

One of the action projects that emerged from a feedback camp was screening films in colleges to build awareness on social issues. The students sourced and selected relevant films, analyzed them, got permission from the colleges, invited students to the screenings, designed and facilitated sessions around the issue. Reflection was a critical piece of the action project as it helped team members to understand the issue at hand and determine their stance before they designed the intervention. After the intervention, they reflected on the process and how it had impacted them, what they could have done better, and how they can improve the project in future. Reflection and action go

Figure 5.7: A Poster for the SMILE Internship Journey

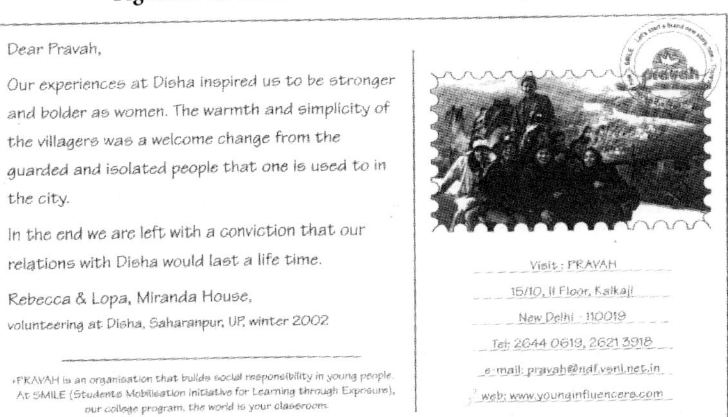

Source: Pravah.

hand in hand and enable young participants to learn more about themselves, develop effective relationships with each other, and impact the larger community. The exposure is a huge turning point for many young people and a great place for transformation. Many young people travel this journey and move on to different careers with sustainable skills to relate with Self and Society as well as the demands of their career choices. This journey supports their decision-making about their life choices in a big way.

We are proud to note that many of our SMILErs have returned to join as youth facilitators within Pravah or in other organizations. Not in token positions either. For example, the current CEO of our direct interventions (Youth Interventions, under which the SMILE program falls, as well as Adolescent Interventions) is a SMILE alumnus. Other SMILE alumni have gone on to become successful media professionals and development sector activists. For example, Inder Pal Singh (SMILE 1998) is today a senior producer at NDTV and brings out a daily puppet show called "Gustakhi Maaf." Bahar Dutt is an environmental editor for CNN-IBN. Bidhan is a planning advisor with Greenpeace. Sunita Menon works for Breakthrough which campaigns against gender-based violence. She is also a member of the Pravah board. While these stories are heartening, we hope to convince the world about the need and success of the 5th Space so as to mainstream the idea of self-development through nation-building in college youth. We are currently in the midst of an extensive, self-driven study to assess the impact of our work over the years.

After a detailed look at one of the 5th Space experiments at Pravah, let's zoom out at the end of this chapter to take a big-picture look at the legitimization of the 5th Space in society.

HOW CAN SOCIETY AS A WHOLE BETTER EMBRACE AND PROMOTE THE 5TH SPACE?

While we have argued earlier that in India the context is not ripe at the moment for the Active Citizenship space to become socially legitimized, we believe there are many developing crises globally that are certainly building a case for young people to be involved in social action.

Unprecedented circumstances unleashed by the consumption model of growth have come together at the beginning of the new millennium, creating a seemingly unsolvable Pamir knot of problems. Added to the global crises of climate change, a worldwide financial meltdown, terrorism, and violent geopolitical tug of wars are India's own insurgencies and development snafus.

All these tragedies are being played out on television and streamed through the four spaces (family, friends, career, and leisure) that young people normally hang out in 24×7×109 (which is the number of current affairs channels at the last count). The common space, in a manner of speaking, is invading the other four. It refuses to be neglected any more.

At the same time many young people have made a mark on the Indian and global stage, and there is a confidence like never before among youth across classes. With the country and the world demanding the intervention of young people and a greater confidence in their ability of playing a decisive part in unraveling the Pamir knot, we believe, the end of the age of cynicism in youth is nigh. The huge involvement of young people in Egypt, Yemen, Syria and, in our own war against corruption, signify that young people are yearning for change and want to participate in ushering it in (see Box 5.5).

Not that all, or even a significant number of young people, will sacrifice their lives—the cause is too vague and too large, and it doesn't have the same emotive feel as the national movement did—but they could be persuaded to engage on their own terms. While some may be inspired to become social activists for life, others (no less activists) could write free software, a few will take to candle light vigils,

Box 5.5: The April 6 Youth Movement, Egypt

This Egyptian facebook group started in 2008 to support textile workers who were planning a strike on April 6 to protest declining wages and rising costs. Within two weeks, its membership expanded to 70,000 young educated people most of whom had never been politically active before. Their core concerns were free speech, nepotism in the government, and a stagnant economy.

"We are all Khaled Saeed!"

This facebook page was set up in 2010 by a group of young cyber activists who were protesting against the brutal murder of 28-year-old Khaled Saeed by the police. It attracted thousands of members within weeks and served as a platform for people to express their anger, discuss tactics of resistance, and organize the 25 January Day of Anger—when Egyptian youth came out en masse to demonstrate against police violence, a corrupt state, and injustice.

Source: Hirschkind 2011; Shokr 2011.

many might join boycotts like the recent cellular silence day and the large majority will be content to merely begin to vote.

We contend that this trickle of Active Citizenship that we are seeing today in India can become a flowing river if we are able to reimagine spaces to which youth throng as 5th Spaces; spaces that enable Self to Society learning and leadership journeys. When 5th Spaces grow far richer than Active Citizenship platforms alone, nourishing other spaces as we outlined before, then we believe society will sanction young people in large numbers to join these 5th Spaces; the river will flood our collective consciousness bringing relief to vast tracts of parched land along its journey to the ocean that stands depleted by the ravages of inequality and overconsumption. It's not even as if we need to create new 5th Spaces from scratch; if we follow the "what" and the "how" suggested in this chapter and imbue all the spaces where young people congregate today with the principles discussed earlier in this chapter, we believe our nation can indeed reap a huge demographic dividend—not only a dividend of economic growth but of human development too.

Not only within India, we feel 5th Spaces can play a great role beyond our borders too. As mentioned earlier, a global mentality is taking shape whose central tenet is that the planet is under siege. In the legend of the Great Deluge (possibly caused by a global warming episode), it was

Figure 5.8: 5th Space Voyages: All Are Welcome Aboard

Source: Authors.

Noah's ark that saved his family and a male and female of every species of the world's animals. The chosen pairs escaped the terrible fate of countless others by taking a voyage on his ship. But to deliver all of humanity, not a chosen few, to a safe place, we cannot depend on one Noah to save us. Rather we must all own up to the Noah in us (see Figure 5.8).

And it would be the 5th Spaces, we have been arguing, which are the crucibles where these new Noahs will be born. We believe it should be society's prime endeavor to promote and nurture these wombs for potential Noahs. In the near future, we hope to see a mushrooming of 5th Spaces similar to the plethora of engineering and MBA colleges we see today. Hopefully, many of these colleges will reimagine themselves as 5th Spaces too. We have argued earlier that the elements of the 5th Space—deep self-awareness, relationship skills, and capacity for engagement with Society—will help young people in their quest for livelihoods, in their dealings with friends and family, and in their leisure and lifestyle choices.

Mainstream education in India is starting to wake up to this reality. It's becoming pretty clear to educators that it is as critical for young people to become more aware of their strengths and passion, be able to handle conflicts, work in teams and become more caring, collaborative leaders, as it is for them to understand the laws of physics and economics and management. This kind of thinking has led to attempts by the Central

Board of Secondary Education (CBSE) in India to incorporate values and life skills education into the current subject syllabi.

Unfortunately, like an organ transplant from a donor with a mismatched blood group, the schools have all but rejected the CBSE initiative. With some notable exceptions, the initiative has turned into a token effort at adding an awareness of societal realities into an already burdened academic curriculum. The recent introduction of the Continuous Comprehensive Evaluation by the CBSE board with its focus on life-skills has only set the cat among the pigeons. Now, schools are supposed to evaluate students on an area they haven't been able to teach well, if at all. In our experience of working with schools they are still struggling to cope with this new move. The hurdles are manifold—ranging from the lack of facilitation skills of current teachers to handling discussions on such delicate, complex issues that raise more questions than provide answers; to integrating issues that have no seeming linkage to current subjects, exam, and syllabus pressures. Parents' expectations from the school for their children and the hugely hierarchical school system add to the difficulties. In our experience, the only way to resolve this situation is by working systemically with schools to create 5th Spaces within, rather than just impose a new life-skills curriculum from above.

Two experiments are currently underway, and we look forward to reporting our learnings from these in another publication. In these experiments, we plan to conduct along with a core group of teachers and students, "whole school appreciative inquiries" that audit a school as a 5th Space and provide an index based on certain parameters which suggest initiatives that the school management, teachers, staff, parents, and students could together take to convert their school into a 5th Space, a space that will nurture "human engineers."

There is also a huge interest in and demand for vocational training in the country today. The government and corporate sector recognize the need for skilled personnel and are willing to invest hugely in this area. The 5th Space can ride this wave adroitly as the livelihoods agenda is like wind in its sails. Currently, curricula in vocational training courses focus on technical skills and skills directly relevant for getting jobs such as interview skills and CV development. A significant value addition to these courses would be to include the 5th Space agenda. Greater self-awareness, stronger relationships skills, and opportunities to apply these skills to social issues will surely help participants to be better workers and entrepreneurs. Another possible widespread introduction of the 5th

Figure 5.9: A Possible 5th Space in a BPO

Source: Authors.

Space could come through the *setting up of youth engagement cells in all organizations.* These cells need not be limited to just NGOs. Young people are a significant part of the workforce of the BPO industry, for example, and youth engagement cells incorporating elements of the 5th Space will directly contribute to their careers and will be welcomed by young people as well as the organizations (see Figure 5.9).

Forming alliances with existing organizations in the youth-development sector and advocating the incorporation of a youth-centric agenda will help build a common understanding and agenda for the sector, and support consolidation. Commutiny—The Youth Collective is such a federation of youth-centric organizations. It was incubated by the Sir Ratan Tata Trusts' Youth and Civil Society initiative and Pravah. As of now it operates as a resource center and advisory board for organizations interested in adopting 5th Space principles within their mainstream work. Two projects are currently underway.

Commutiny—The Youth Collective also realizes that youth voices and youth perspectives are largely absent in the media and given the huge outreach and influence of the media today, we feel the need to find creative ways of *using media as an advocacy tool to promote the 5th Space.* Currently, the Youth Collective has created a media network where young grassroots activists are engaged in developing products on youth leadership in their communities. Additionally, it has also commissioned well-known media experts in film and print to promote the concept of 5th Space among architects and navigators of youth spaces (see Box 5.6). At the Youth Collective, the main thrust is to become a think tank of 5th Space designers. In every board meeting (once in 45 days) either member organizations or others wishing to create 5th Spaces for young people are encouraged to bring their challenges to the collective drawing board. Applying the collective years of experience around the table to each challenge, we believe, enriches the design a lot and adds to the quality and quantity of 5th Spaces on the ground.

Box 5.6: Creative Media and Policy Group

An Initiative of Commutiny—The Youth Collective

Using diverse media from grassroots to mainstream, Commutiny—The Youth Collective is engaging with select stakeholders from the media, civil society organizations, youth, and the larger civil society to build visibility and appreciation of youth issues. It has established the Commutiny Media Network (CMN) to learn how to use media to express youth voices. CMN builds capacities of youth activists and youth facilitators from 12 organizations across the country who use media to express their views, function in media spaces, and strengthen their work with communities on youth issues. Achievements of this network range from coverage in regional media to conducting research on relevant youth issues and youth-led comics campaigns. A set of mainstream media fellows are also being appointed who will link up with the grassroots network and produce youth leadership stories for their own electronic or print media publication.

An online and offline campaign on gender (with a special focus on masculinity) is underway that is co-led with a core group of youth. Called Must Bol, this campaign has effectively utilized social media and workshops to create a huge buzz in college campuses in Delhi.

Source: Compiled by the authors.

Finally we would like to turn to the government and policymakers and what could be done by them to promote a more youth-centric agenda. We had argued earlier in Chapter 2 that after the Independence movement, the government has typically approached the young people's ocean with a spoon and thus reduced it to a drop. Not only does the Ministry of Youth Affairs need more young people in leadership positions, we believe it must play a more central role in the implementation strategies of all the ministries.

The creation of a separate Ministry of Youth Affairs and Sports was a much needed positive declaration of intent. But this is not the only ministry that deals with young people. The Ministry of Human Resource Development and its Department of Education, Ministry of Health and Family Welfare, Ministry of Labour and Employment, Ministry of Social Justice and Empowerment, and Ministry of Women and Child Development are a few key ministries that have and must include schemes for young people. The National Youth Policy of 2003 recognizes that

> an inter-sectoral approach is a pre-requisite for dealing with youth-related issues. It, therefore, advocates the establishment of a coordinating mechanism among the various Central Government Ministries and Departments and between the Central and State Governments, and community-based organisations and youth bodies for facilitating convergence in youth-related schemes, developing integrated policy initiatives for youth programmes and for reviewing on-going activities/ schemes to fill in gaps and remove unnecessary duplication and overlap. ("National Youth Policy 2003," available at http://www.youth-policy.com/ policies/ [downloaded on November 7, 2012]) (See Figure 5.10.)

It would be interesting to examine what mechanisms are in place to make this happen and how well they are functioning. One way to ensure this structurally is for the Youth Ministry to become a nodal agency that interacts with and integrates government schemes and programs for young people across all ministries and government departments, as has been shown in Figure 5.11.

Another option could be for each of the ministries to have a dedicated Youth Cell that connects with the Ministry of Youth Affairs and their schemes—NYKS and NSS—both of which have widespread outreach

Figure 5.10: The Need for Genuine Youth Involvement in Policymaking

Source: Authors.

Figure 5.11: Ministry of Youth Affairs—A Cross-cutting Ministry

Ministry of HRD	Ministry of Health and Family Welfare	Ministry of Social Justice and Empowerment	Ministry of Women and Child Development
Ministry of Youth Affairs: A Cross-cutting Ministry with representation from each ministry working with youth			

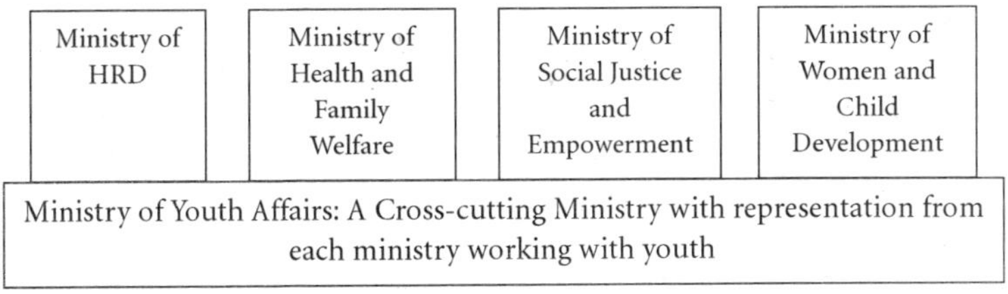

Source: Authors.

and decent infrastructure. While they have laudable objectives with a strong focus on youth development, quality of implementation is often patchy. By *developing partnerships with NYKS and NSS programs and using this experience to advocate for the reform of NYKS and NSS* so as to ensure the integration of elements of the 5th Space, we could make a significant impact on the large numbers of young people these programs can reach out to. Also the Rajiv Gandhi National Institute for Youth Development (RGNIYD)—the nodal agency of the Ministry—is currently building its capacities and in future there will be promising opportunities to undertake collaborative initiatives and research. Another encouraging development is the introduction of postgraduate courses on youth development by a range of institutions, such as Nirmala Niketan, Indira Gandhi National Open University (IGNOU), Commonwealth Youth Program Asia (CYPA), and Rajiv Gandhi National Institute of Youth Development (RGNIYD).

Finally, we would like to remind policymakers that the nation would be better served by encouraging young people to discover the ocean within them, rather than telling them to only contribute their drop in the project of nation building.

CHAPTER HIGHLIGHTS

In this chapter, we have outlined a few principles that govern the contours of the 5th Space. Ownership is the first of these principles. The second looks at who is in charge of the space. We advocate that the spaces be youth-led and yet it's critical that there are trained, unbiased facilitators available who can support young people through the stages of group development. Next, we speak of the principle of helping the young to move from the known to the unknown; so we recommend that we start with the Self and then gradually turn their gaze on Society. Also it is important to identify markers and measures for all the important components of the journey, that is, for Self, skills to relate and impact on Society. Another principle talks of the character or *sifat* promoting trust, "cross-border" friendships, a safe place to hang out, and joyful engagement. Finally the 5th Space balances the "Now" of young people with the "Future" obsession of society. This means creating opportunities for the feelings and emotional side of the young person to flourish, which can only be in the present, is as critical as the purpose and tasks. Thus, the space should be able to empathize with and heal an inhabitant who may not be feeling positive and thus could wreck the space by his/her negative energy. Lastly, a 5th Space needs to be able to renew itself when its founders leave without having to start from scratch again.

We moved on from the principles to outline the ideal process model for the 5th Space—one which draws upon the various theories that relate to youthhood. A case study of Pravah's current experiments with the SMILE program as a 5th Space was shared. In SMILE, as in other programs, we have been able to tie the three areas of Self, relationships, and Society together using interventions called the Conflict Positive and Get Real. Viewing society as a connected open system, we position conflict as the catalyzer of change rather than merely a problem to resolve. We believe that conflict between the "differences" in a system create the necessary energy for the system to self-organize from a status quo to a system at a higher level. It is only when the actors in the conflict resort to violence that the conflict becomes undesirable. Therefore, when they apply the steps of conflict positive to their own personal conflict and to a social one they learn about self (taking stances based on their values), gain leadership skills (especially consensus-building), and knowledge about the issue.

In the last section of this chapter, we made some key recommendations that would help society as a whole to embrace and promote the 5th Space. These range from creating 5th Spaces in the livelihood and vocational training institutions to changes in the structuring of ministries to getting the youth affairs ministry to function as a cross-functional aid for all the other ministries. Recommendations also include using media as an advocacy tool to promote the 5th Space, whole school reimagination of educational institutions as 5th Spaces and a consolidation of the youth development sector under a collective youth-centric agenda.

Epilogue
The World Is My Classroom

[.... Continued from the Prologue]

Even in these career-oriented times, some time, not too far into the future, we hope to hear this kind of a conversation.

The mobile rings. "Where are you?" a male voice asks.

She answers, "Where else? You ask the same question every day."

"I keep hoping I'll get a different answer. So, on your way to class?"

"School in the morning and medical coaching classes in the evening. From one classroom to another. That's all I seem to do; as if my world is limited to the classroom."

"Break out of the prison today! There's this new hangout—something called a Youth Adda near the Khamekha Mall. I read about it in the Friday *Times*. Remember Avinash—he's from your school, that good-looking guy. Two to three years senior to you. He's showing a documentary film on Kabir. Supposed to be a great film—read somewhere that it helps you think about yourself and all that. Also, we can talk to the facilitator about that organic food stall you wanted to run at your school fest."

"I do really want to learn more about how pesticides and chemical fertilizers harm our health. Nobody in school seems to know enough about it. Even the teachers tell me to look it up on the Internet. One would think that those students interested in a medical career would want to know about organic food produced without pesticides. But no, they just go on studying about disease."

"As if a doc's job is only to cure."

"Yes, prevention is not a doctor's headache, it seems."

"Ah prevention! I read that this group which has started the Youth Adda I was telling you about; believes in prevention. It is their preferred approach even for social diseases like poverty."

"Huh? The only way I know how to prevent poverty is to get a fat salary as a doctor in a super specialty hospital. Which is why I don't think it's a good idea to go to this Youth Adda today; so please don't try to prevent me from going to my class."

"Else you will end up as a poor nurse...."

""... like Mom! Ya, it's her most pressing fear ... which is why you know she doesn't like me missing classes."

"True, she is so keen to see you become a doctor. She will be devastated if you don't get through."

"You know Mom ... she doesn't like me coming home late."

"But this is different. We aren't fooling around or anything. Don't worry I'll talk to her."

"She always waits up for dinner...."

"We'll tell her not to worry about dinner; they serve really cool *vada*s made from organically grown *sabudana* at the Adda's café. C'mon it'll be fun."

"Actually, to be honest it does sound awesome!"

"So are you coming?"

"But what about my coaching class, *Papa*?"

"How can you be a doctor without knowing more about organic food? You only said that doctors should learn prevention strategies and not only cure. Think of the world as your classroom, girl."

"But Papa, prevention is not going to come in the exams! Also the main session in the Youth Adda is about self-awareness you said. What's that got to do with education?"

"Everything! The newspapers quoted the VC of Delhi University as saying that learning is only knowledge till you relate it to yourself. He teaches math, and he says he tells his students to apply all his teaching in their real life and forget whatever they can't. He's right! Education should start in our feet and move up to our head rather than the other way round. Only then does it become learning."

"By the way, why are you so insistent Papa? What's in it for you?"

"Well who else will facilitate this experimentation for you? And who knows, I might meet somebody interesting while hanging out with you in the Adda.... Actually, to be quite honest, they had a picture of the Adda's facilitator in the article. Turns out I knew her from college. Aditi."

"Ah, I see what you are trying to do Papa. I'm a bait for bigger fish."

"No thanks! I've got my fish waiting for me at home. I'm a one fish man. Please don't teach me how to fish at this late stage in life. In fact, it's your age to fish and Avinash is not a bad sort.... And while you are at it, I wouldn't mind sitting by the banks and swapping stories with Aditi."

"Okay Pops, I agree to give you cover as you sit with Aditi on the banks. We'll see about the fish, but I'll catch you at the Khameka Mall in half an hour. Do let mom know in the meanwhile."

Annexure 1

Contours of the Study

The ocean in the drop—A perspective on youth ownership of common spaces

Youth have been engaged in social action with varying intensity through our country's history. Most narrators would no doubt locate this social action at its highest during the Independence movement. Then it appears to have dipped for the next few decades as young people were excluded from the process of nation building and governance. It rose again in the sixties and seventies with the establishment of several NGOs and social movements, such as the Sarvodaya movement, JP's student movement, the Naxalite movement, etc., only to ebb substantially in the neo-liberal nineties, when careers and the India growth story captured the imagination of the country. Now in the first decade of this century, we feel we are once again witnessing a renewed engagement of young people with social issues fuelled maybe by a collapse of ideologies and multiple crises looming large.

In an attempt to analyze these trends of youth engagement in social action, we set out to test the following two hypotheses:

1. *A conducive environment and context pulls in youth to participate actively in civil society.*
2. *Social action by youth transforms young people as much as it changes the world around them.*

The objectives of this study were:

1. uncover the basic systemic elements that encourage and facilitate youth social action and those which act as barriers to it;
2. conceptualize an alternative dynamic that will allow mainstreaming

of youth engaged in social action, thereby enabling their own identity formation as strong citizens and better human beings; and
3. recommend possible strategies and entry points for organizations working or wishing to work with young people.

METHODOLOGY

To do the above, we built on the experience and expertise of Pravah, Oxfam India and its partners, and also undertook primary and secondary research. Other partners in this process were the Strategic Resource Group (SRG)[1] and Association for Stimulating Know how (ASK)[2] who partnered in the primary and secondary research we conducted.

The research included: *(a)* review of Nehru Memorial Museum and Library (NMML) oral history transcripts of youth in the forties; *(b)* interviews about life in the forties with 30 people currently between the ages of 80 and 90; *(c)* interviews with key stakeholders such as sociologists/historians and organizations/institutions that work with young people; *(d)* review of the forties' editions of newspapers, such as *Young India* and the *Student* read by youth and other primary literature written by student leaders of the forties, and *(e)* review of secondary literature on students movements in India.

[1]SRG was a collaborative effort between The Youth and Civil Society Initiative of Sir Ratan Tata Trust and Pravah, set up to strengthen youth development and Active Citizenship.

[2]ASK, established in 1993, is a capacity-building organization that engages with grassroots communities, NGOs, government, and corporates to enhance reflection, learrning, and action to achieve equitable development and social justice.

Annexure 2

List of Key Informants

S. No	Persons met	Designation	Agency
1.	Mr C. S. Pran	Director—Program	Nehru Yuvak Kendra Sangathan
2.	Dr Babli Moitra Saraf	Principal	Indraprastha College
3.	Dr Sanjay Kumar	Fellow	Centre for Social Development Studies (CSDS)
4.	Mr Amit Malik	President	Delhi Pradesh Youth Congress
5.	Reverend Valson Thampu	Principal	St. Stephen's College
6.	Dr Suroopa Mukherjee	Teacher, English Literature and Coordinator of B for Bhopal campaign	Hindu College
7.	Mr Kedar Nath Sahni	Member	Bhartiya Janata Party (Ex Governor, Goa)
8.	Dr Karan Singh	Chairman, Foreign Affairs Cell	Indian National Congress

(Annexure 2 Continued)

(Annexure 2 Continued)

S. No	Persons met	Designation	Agency
9.	Mr Milin Oke	Volunteer, Delhi Unit	Rashtriya Swayam Sevak Sangh
10.	Mr Ashim Roy	Secretary	New Trade Union of India (NTUI)
11.	Professor Mukul Manglik	Associate Professor, Department of History	Ramjas College
12.	Professor Satish Deshpande	Professor, Center of Advanced Studies	Department of Sociology, Delhi School of Economics
13.	Father Alwyn D'Souza	Executive Secretary	Youth Commission, Catholic Bishop Conference of India
14.	Mr Girish Tuteja	Program Advisor	National Service Scheme
15.	Dr Lata Narayan	Associate Professor, Center for Equity for Women, Children and Families	School of Social Work, Tata Institute of Social Sciences
16.	Ms Rama Shyam	Coordinator	SAHER, Mumbai
17.	Mr K. T. Suresh	Executive Director	YUVA Collective, Mumbai
18.	Mr Maninder Singh	Sevadar	Bangla Sahib Gurudwara
19.	Professor Meenakshi Thapan	Professor	Department of Sociology, Delhi School of Economics

Annexure 3

Oral Transcripts of Youth in the Forties Who Engaged in Social Action

	Name	Year of birth	Place of birth	Social action
1.	Dr Mrs Shanti Ghosh	1920	Srinagar	Relief worker during the Bengal Famine.
2.	M. K. Johry	1921	Mathura	Took part in 1942 Quit India revolutionary activities (burning cinemas, post offices and dacoity). Imprisoned for dacoity. Influence of family and nationalist feelings.
3.	Sehdev Kapoor	1924	Gurdaspur	Took part in Quit India Movement (1942). Arrested for his antiwar activities and imprisoned for three and a half years. Family imbued with nationalist feelings.

(Annexure 3 Continued)

(Annexure 3 Continued)

	Name	Year of birth	Place of birth	Social action
4.	Dr Usha Mehta	1920	Saras (Surat)	Participated in the Quit India Movement (1942) and worked with the underground Congress radio. Arrested.
5.	Mrs Madalsa Sriman Narayan	1917	Wardha	Closely associated with Gandhi and Vinoba Bhave because of her parents (Jamnalal Bajaj and Janki Devi). Educated in Gandhi's ashrams. Burnt foreign clothes, participated in Quit India Movement. (Dandi March, *Harijan* tour).
6.	G. P. Nene	1913	Varanasi	Took part in the Quit India Movement. Influenced by national leaders.
7.	Ishwarbhai J. Patel	1914	Kheda district, Gujarat	Took part in Dandi March. Did plague work in 1934–1935. Resigned as principal of D. N. High School, Anand, and organized underground activities during the Quit India Movement.
8.	Meherchand Ahuja	1912	Cambalpur	Active in the Independence Movement since childhood, arrested several times, influenced by communism, participated in the Quit India Movement, member of the executive council of the Punjab CSP.

	Name	Year of birth	Place of birth	Social action
9.	Arjun Arora	1912	Kanpur	Influenced by Chandrashekhar Azad. Arrested while trying to make a bomb when in Class 10, later veered toward communism, held office in various positions in trade unions.
10.	Dev Dutt Atal	1913	Muzzafargarh	Actively involved in the Independence Movement, imprisoned several times, influenced by the protests following the arrival of the Simon Commission in early youth, and participated in the Goa liberation movement.
11.	Sadashiv Bagailkar	1923	Junnar, Pune	Worked for eliminating untouchability and struggle for labor and peasant empowerment, participated in the Quit India Movement and was imprisoned for three and a half years, as well as post-Independence for participating in labor movements and political activism; also participated in Goan and Bangladeshi liberation movements.
12.	Bhagwandas	1917	Rohtak district	Participated in the Civil Disobedience Movement in 1930 and 1932, arrested, involved

(Annexure 3 Continued)

(Annexure 3 Continued)

	Name	Year of birth	Place of birth	Social action
				in the khadi movement, Rajasthan and Punjab Charkha Sangh, participated in individual Satyagraha, Quit India Movement, arrested several times, worked for khadi promotion, sarvodaya and cow protection post-Independence.
13.	Aurobindo Bose	1921	Calcutta	Subhas Chandra Bose's nephew. Joined Bengal volunteers in 1935, led students' strike in college, organized students agitation for repatriation of Andaman's political prisoners (1938). Held leadership positions in All India Students Federation and All India Students Congress. Worked with Gandhi during communal disturbances in Calcutta, Noakhali, and Bihar (1947).
14.	Praful Chaudhuri	1913	Noakhali	Influenced by Anushilan Samiti. Joined Revolutionary Socialist Party.
15.	Brahm Prakash Chaudhuri	1918	Delhi	Arrested four times for participating in the national movement, was general secretary of

	Name	Year of birth	Place of birth	Social action
				Delhi Pradesh Congress Committee (DPCC) from 1946 to 1951, chief minister of Delhi for three years, imprisoned during Emergency for participating in JP's movement.
16.	Hitendra K. Desai	1915	Surat	Joined Congress. Participated in Bardoli Satyagraha, Salt Satyagraha, Quit India Movement. Imprisoned. (Later became chief minister of Gujarat and member of Lok Sabha.)
17.	Yash Dev Dharam	1911	Mianwali (Pakistan)	Took part in anti-Simon Commission procession in Lahore, member of Lahore students union.
18.	Banu Ram Gupta	1921	Shahabad, Haryana	Participated in the Hyderabad Satyagraha and imprisoned for six months, Quit India Movement and imprisonment, member of Punjab Pradesh Congress committee post- Independence, social work.
19.	Vinayak Kulkarni	1914	Poona	Involvement in Quit India Movement in the Kolhapur princely state, imprisoned, worked for

(Annexure 3 Continued)

(Continued Annexure 3)

	Name	Year of birth	Place of birth	Social action
				labor rights in Pune, participated in the Goan liberation movement.
20.	Giani Meher Singh	1915	Amritsar	Influenced by the sacrifice of Baba Vir Singh and Maharaj Singh, secretary of district congress committee of 24-Parganas, Bengal, from 1937 to 1938, arrested and fined in 1938, involved in religious and social work bodies after Independence.
21.	Asoka Mehta	1911	Bhavnagar	Participated in the Civil Disobedience and Quit India Movements and imprisoned for several years. Founder member of the Congress Socialist Party. Later became member, Lok Sabha and union minister.
22.	Bhela Paswan Shastri	1911	Purniya, Bihar	Involved in the national movement since student days, imprisoned several times, was chief minister of Bihar in 1968, 1969, and 1971.
23.	Frederick Michael Pinto	1912	Mangalore	Participated in freedom struggle and imprisoned. Founder member of Congress Socialist Party.
24.	Prabodh Chandra	1911	Rawalpindi	Actively involved in the national movement and

	Name	Year of birth	Place of birth	Social action
				student activism, member of "krantikari bal," influenced by the ideology of Bhagat Singh and his friends, was the head of All India Students Conference in 1936, MP from 1971 to 1977.
25.	Mrs Prakashwati Pal	1914	Amritsar	Ran away from home. Participation in revolutionary activities from 1928 onward, imprisoned for a fortnight in 1934 and barred from entering Delhi for a year, was involved in the Jhandewalan bomb factory during revolutionary days.
26.	Ramavtar Shastri	1920	Patna	Actively involved in student unions, member of the Indian National Congress from 1930 to 1945, joined the Communist Party later, was in prison for about a decade during the Independence Movement and for more than three years post-Independence.
27.	Hargobind Ramchandani	1924	Karachi	Participated in the Quit India Movement and imprisoned for three months. Issued several bogus governmental orders in 1942–1943.

(Annexure 3 Continued)

(Annexure 3 Continued)

	Name	Year of birth	Place of birth	Social action
28.	Ranbir Singh Chaudhury	1914	Rohtak	Imprisoned eight times between 1941 and 1946 for involvement in the national movement, was the congress whip in the Lok Sabha and a minister in Punjab and Haryana post-Independence.
29.	P. Sundarayya	1913	Nellore district	Boycott of Simon Commission (1928), formation of communist group at Loyola College (1929), arrested (1930), joined Communist Party (1931–1932), kisan struggle against zamindars (1936–1939), social service in Andhra villages. Later became member of Rajya Sabha and leadership position in CPI-M.
30.	Ishwardas Talwar	1913	NWFP	Brother of the martyr Hari Kishan who was heavily influenced by Bhagat Singh. His other brother, Bhagatram Talwar, was instrumental in Subhash Chandra Bose's escape to Kabul, was imprisoned several times during the national movement and the entire family suffered immense hardship for involvement in the national movement and was reduced to poverty.

	Name	Year of birth	Place of birth	Social action
31.	Pratap K. Tandon	1924	Lucknow	Participated in the Quit India Movement. Active worker of All India Students Federation (AISF) (BHU) and later its secretary (Uttar Pradesh). Imprisoned. Went underground to work with peasants in Uttar Pradesh.
32.	Narayan Mulram Wadhwani	1924	Sukkur, Sind	Attended Salt Satyagraha meetings and was lathi charged (1930), joined Swaraj Sena Mandal (1938), active member of AISF, organized students strike in Sukkur. Arrested during the Quit India Movement for cutting telephone wires and imprisoned for three years.
33.	Captain Ramsingh Thakur	1914	Dharamshala, Himachal Pradesh	Joined the Indian army, entered the ranks of the Indian National Army in the forties, became the music director and got the rank of captain, arrested by the British government in 1945, organized the Indian National Army (INA) orchestra after release, got several national honors as a great singer of the national song. Inspired the soldiers through his songs.

(Annexure 3 Continued)

(Annexure 3 Continued)

	Name	Year of birth	Place of birth	Social action
34.	Jamutlal Yadav	1919	Rajasthan	Observed the work of Arya Samaj in and around Ajmer, met Gandhiji for the first time in 1934, worked with the Harijan Sewak Sangh, involved in movement against the Mewar princely state and imprisoned for it, involved in the Quit India Movement, minister in Rajasthan government post-Independence.
35.	Shahnawaz Khan	1914	Rawalpindi district	Joined the INA under Subash Chandra Bose. Later became member of Lok Sabha and minister.
36.	Jagat Ram Sahni	1918	NWFP	Participated in the Quit India Movement and imprisoned for two years.
37.	Mathuradas Mathur	1918	Jodhpur	Took part in the Quit India Movement and jailed in 1940 and 1942.
38.	Amarnath Malhotra	1919	Peshawar	Actively involved in the national movement since childhood, arrested at the age of 11 for breaking the Salt Law, whipped, arrested in 1937 for distributing illegal literature, imprisoned for four years in the forties, joined the communist party after release.

	Name	Year of birth	Place of birth	Social action
39.	Acharya Lakshmi Raman	1917		Took part in the Independence Movement, imprisoned in connection with the Agra conspiracy case and during the Quit India Movement. Later became member of Legislative Assembly (MLA) and minister.
40.	Mohamed Raza Khan	1912	Madras	One of the pioneers who organized the Muslim league in Madras. Member of the All India Muslim League Council (1943–1948).
41.	D. R. Handa	1913	Lahore	Involved in revolutionary action, was part of the efforts to get Bhagat Singh released, participated in the June 19, 1930 action to explode bombs in six towns in Panjab, imprisoned for three years.
42.	Bhogibhai Gandhi	1911	Gujarat	Participated in Bardoli Satyagraha (1928) and went to jail several times in 1930–1934.
43.	Dr Fateh Chand	1914	NWFP	Involved in Harijan empowerment as a student, worked for rural development and as a congressman during college days, expelled

(Annexure 3 Continued)

(Annexure 3 Continued)

	Name	Year of birth	Place of birth	Social action
				from college, arrested during the Quit India Movement, worked for communal harmony, engaged in refugee rehabilitation post Partition.
44.	Vanamala Desai	1922	Ahmedabad	Educated in Sabarmati Ashram. Participated in Champaran Satyagraha, Dandi March, individual satyagraha and the India Movement, imprisoned four times between 1941 and 1942.
45.	Y. B. Chavan	1913		Participated in the Civil Disobedience Movement (1932) and was imprisoned for his political activities. Directed underground movement in Satara district.
46.	Chamanlal Batra	1916	Panjab	Imprisoned for four months as a student for picketing in front of liqor shops, helped in organization of congress committees in villages, participated in "Moga agitation," arrested for individual satyagraha and the Quit India Movement, involved in

	Name	Year of birth	Place of birth	Social action
				refugee rehabilitation and in various congress committees post-Independence.
47.	Gopalrao A. Ekbote	1912	Hyderabad	Participated in Satyagraha movement.
48.	H. Heda	1912	Osmanabad district	Influenced by Tilak and Gandhi. Secretary of Hyderabad Harijan Sevak Sangh (1930–1938). Took active part in the Independence Movement in Hyderabad and imprisoned.
49.	Bir Madhav	1922	Goa	Left studies to participate in the Quit India Movement. Participated in the Goa freedom struggle.
50.	R. P. Puri	1920	Hoshiarpur	Took part in the Quit India Movement in Delhi, including abortive plan to demolish King George's statue, the burning of Statesman godown and Jamuna Canal robbery. Imprisoned.
51.	Col. Prem Kumar Sehgal	1917	Hoshiarpur	INA—closely associated with Subhash Chandra Bose.
52.	Dr Mrs Lakshmi Sahgal	1914	Madras	Joined INA in 1943 and organized its women's unit.

(Annexure 3 Continued)

(Annexure 3 Continued)

	Name	Year of birth	Place of birth	Social action
53.	Manubhai Mansukhlal Shah	1915	Gujarat	Took part in the Quit India Movement in Delhi, including underground activities, such as robbery at Metcalfe house, damaging of All India Radio station, derailment of Frontier Mail, throwing of bombs on British shops, burning of currency notes in front of Reserve Bank of India, breaking King George statue, killing of police inspector. Imprisoned in Red Fort.

Annexure 4

List of Octogenarians Interviewed

	Name	Sex	Year of birth	Region	Education	Profession
1.	Mr H. S. Chatterji	M	1926	Dhaka	Graduate	Government
2.	Mrs Kushal Garg	F	1926	Lahore	Postgraduate	Homemaker
3.	Mr B. M. Chopra	M	1927	Lahore	Graduate	Private sector
4.	Mr Shyam Lal Verma	M	1928	Punjab	Matric	Railways
5.	Mr S. P. Ghai	M	1929	Kashmir	Matric	Business
6.	Mr K. C. Hasija	M	1929	Punjab	Graduate	Railways
7.	Mr S. P. Sagar	M	1927	Punjab	Postgraduate	Bank
8.	Mr S. P. Roy	M	1929	Bihar	Graduate	Government
9.	Mr K. N. Sahni	M	1926	Punjab	Graduate	Social organization
10.	Mrs Helen Singh	F	1929	Uttar Pradesh	MBBS	Government health
11.	Mrs Dhanwanti	F	1928	Haryana	Nonliterate	Homemaker

(Annexure 4 Continued)

(Annexure 4 Continued)

	Name	Sex	Year of birth	Region	Education	Profession
12.	Mr Satya Prakash	M	1927	Haryana	Matric	Government
13.	Mr Anand Swaroop	M	1929	Punjab	Graduate	Government
14.	Sheonarayan	F	1924	Haryana	Nonliterate	Farmer
15.	Mr Baldev Mahendroo	M	1928	Punjab	Graduate	Government
16.	Lt. General M. L. Yadav	M	1928	Haryana	Graduate	Army
17.	Mrs Janaki Khileni	F	1926	Delhi	Graduate	Homemaker
18.	Mr S. C. Basu	M	1932	Bengal	Graduate	Government
19.	Mr Om Prakash	M	1930	Lahore	Engineering	Private sector
20.	Mr R. N. Bhatnagar	M	1925	Rajasthan	Engineering	Private sector
21.	Lt. General S. K. Sinha	M	1926	Bihar	Graduate	Army
22.	Mrs Niroo Mahapatra	F	1929	Orissa	Graduate	Artist
23.	Mrs Shakuntala Mehra	F	1927	Delhi	Postgraduate	College lecturer
24.	Dr Bina Roy Burman	F	1929	Calcutta	Postgraduate	Researcher
25.	Mr M. B. Lal	M	1929	Uttar Pradesh	Graduate	Journalist
26.	Mr M. M. Bhatnagar	M	1927	Kanpur	Graduate	Public sector
27.	Mrs Kochar	F	1930	Ambala	12th grade	Homemaker
28.	Mrs Kamla Rai	F	1921	Karachi	Graduate	Homemaker
29.	Mrs Tarawati	F	1923	Delhi	No formal schooling	Homemaker
30.	Mrs Bimla Sharma	F	1921	Uttar Pradesh	Postgraduate	Educationalist

Annexure 5

Findings of the Study

Participation in social action

How many times did you participate in any demonstration, struggle, or movements	Total	
	In numbers	In percentage
Never	20	66.6
Once or twice	2	6.6
Several times	8	26.6
Grand Total	**30**	**100.00**

How much time did you spend on a average in the space of social action/ Active Citizenship (in percentage)	Total	
	In numbers	In percentage
0	18	60
10–20	7	23.3
80	5	16.6
Grand Total	**30**	**100.00**

If you did not take part in engaging with issues, can you tell us why?	Total	
	In numbers	In perccentage
Busy with family responsibilities	5	16.6
Did not participate due to social constraints	1	3.3
Fear	1	3.3
More focus on job	3	10
Parents forbade it	4	13.3
Not available	11	36.67
No exposure/awareness	3	10
No response	2	6.6
Grand Total	**30**	**100.00**

What was important in life?

What do you thing was important for you as a youth, good career, or social action?	Total	
	In numbers	In percentage
Family	2	6.67
Good career	18	60
Social action	5	16.67
Neither	3	10
Both	2	6.67
Grand Total	**30**	**100.00**

Getting higher education	Total	
	In numbers	In percentage
Less important	3	10
Not important	4	13.3
Quite important	10	33.3
Very important	13	43.33
Grand Total	**30**	**100.00**

Getting married	Total	
	In numbers	In percentage
Not so important	10	33.3
Quite important	5	16.67
Somewhat important	7	23.3
Very important	8	26.6
Grand Total	**30**	**100.00**

Taking on responsibility	Total	
	In numbers	In percentage
Less important	5	16.6
Quite important	5	16.6
Very important	20	66.6
Grand Total	**30**	**100.00**

Influences

Friends as influence	Total	
	In numbers	In percentage
Great deal	6	20.00
Not very much	16	53.3
Quite some	8	26.6
Grand Total	**30**	**100.00**

Parents as influence	Total	
	In numbers	In percentage
Great deal	18	60
Not much	4	13.3
Quite some	6	20
Grand Total	**30**	**100.00**

Teachers as influence	Total	
	In numbers	In percentage
Great deal	9	30
None	7	23.3
Not very much	10	33.3
Quite some	4	13.3
Grand Total	**30**	**100.00**

Political leaders as influence	Total	
	In numbers	In percentage
Great deal	14	46.67
None	3	10
Not much	7	23.3
No response	1	3.3
Quite some	5	16.6
Grand Total	**30**	**100.00**

Cross-border friendships

Did you have friends from different religions	Total	
	In numbers	In percentage
No	4	13.3
Yes	26	86.6
Grand Total	**30**	**100.00**

Did you have friends from different caste?	Total	
	In numbers	In percentage
Not available	1	3.3
No response	1	3.3

Did you have friends from different caste?	Total	
	In numbers	**In percentage**
Not aware of caste	2	6.6
Yes	20	66.67
No	6	20
Grand Total	**30**	**100.00**

Did you have friends of the opposite sex?	Total	
	In numbers	**In percentage**
No	20	66.6
Yes	10	33.3
Grand Total	**30**	**100.00**

Profile of respondents

Age	Total	
	In numbers	**In percentage**
78	1	3.3
80	2	6.6
81	8	26.6
82	4	13.3
83	5	16.6
84	5	16.6
85	1	3.3
86	1	3.3
87	1	3.3
89	1	3.3
92	1	3.3
Grand Total	**30**	**100.00**

Sex	Total	
	In numbers	In percentage
Female	11	36.6
Male	19	63.3
Grand Total	**30**	**100.00**

Education	Total	
	In numbers	In percentage
Graduate	15	50
No formal schooling	3	10.00
Matric	4	13.3
Postgraduate	8	26.6
Grand Total	**30**	**100.00**

Employment	Total	
	In numbers	In percentage
Army	2	6.6
Bank	1	3.3
Business	1	3.3
Farmer	1	3.3
Government	8	26.6
Homemaker	7	23.3
Railways	2	6.6
Private sector	3	5
Social organization	1	3.3
Academics	3	5
Journalist	1	3.3
Grand Total	**30**	**100.00**

Annexure 6

Competencies and Indicators for Impact Assessment of Youth Interventions

A. SELF-REALIZATION AND EXPRESSION		
Parameters	**Competencies (KSAB)**[1]	**Indicators**
A 1. Self-awareness	Ability to see Self-critically	Percentage of time and reflective space for self-exploration
	Ability to analyze my identity and be comfortable with multiple identities Ability to assess and articulate one's strengths, personality traits, areas of improvements, prejudices, comfort zones, traits Ability to prioritize my life goals	Articulation of given and constructed identities and comfort zones Examples of questioning and negotiation of boundaries—identity, role, relationships, goals variations in Self-concept, and others' perceptions Articulation of goals and vision

(Annexure 6 Continued)

[1] Knowledge, Skills, Attitudes, Behaviors.

(Annexure 6 Continued)

Parameters	Competencies (KSAB)	Indicators
	Ability to locate myself in the world and my vision of the world Ability to identify personal vulnerabilities and prioritize well-being for enhancing productivity and happiness	Articulation and analysis of shifts in goals and in my journey
A 2. Self-esteem and confidence	Humility Ability to express one's views in public Resilience	Number of perceived risk experiences Number of times one has failed and moved on
	Locus of control: Shift from external to internal locus	Identification of personal capacity to handle situations and take responsibility for decisions
	Ability to take informed stances/ choices based on one's values Ability to change my stances	Articulation of multiple points of view Demonstrated understanding of the values and rationale informing my stance/ choice Number of times I have withstood peer/societal pressure Number of times and experiences of challenging existing frameworks and finding creative alternatives to address social and personal challenges (including marriage and career)

Parameters	Competencies (KSAB)	Indicators
A 3. Learnability/ Learning	Ability to learn from my own and others' experiences (including mistakes, successes, setbacks)	Articulation of lessons learned Frequency of course correction based on reflection and lessons learned
	Ability to seek feedback and work on it Ability to learn from different sources using different learning styles	Number of times I have sought and responded to feedback Number of learning opportunities proactively created/ sought Number of experiences outside my learning style/comfort zone Number of times I have challenged myself
	Ability to recognize one's call/passion and follow it Ability to develop one's own learning plan, reflect and monitor progress	Articulation of learning needs Frequency of revisiting learning plan
	Ability to ask appropriate questions	Frequency of asking appropriate questions that: • add to creative knowledge • are challenging • create engagement
A 4. Expression	Ability to celebrate life—sense of optimism, energy, joy, happiness, fulfillment, achievement Ability to love and trust	Examples of celebrations and positive stories

(Annexure 6 Continued)

(Annexure 6 Continued)

Parameters	Competencies (KSAB)	Indicators
	Ability to gauge, express, and manage one's emotions	Examples of expressing emotions authentically and demonstrating positive change while dealing with it objectively
A 5. Interpret and create new stories	Ability to understand, analyze and construct meaning, and communicate it effectively	Frequency of original/ authentic/honest interpretations
A. 6 Lifestyles	Time and money management Ability to choose healthy lifestyles (physical, emotional, and mental, as well as climate-conscious and sustainable) Ability to choose a viable livelihood combining passion and need	Options explored and livelihood option found Sense of financial security, productive engagement with livelihood

B. INTERPERSONAL RELATIONSHIPS

Parameters	Competencies	Indicators
B 1. Respect and empathy	Ability to create a safe space and initiate a dialogue (respect, humility, nonjudgmental, approachable) Ability to imagine another person's feelings (sensing)	Number and quality of relationships Recognition of others' needs Frequency of initiatives taken to initiate dialogue Examples of sharing/ dialogue (around personal and taboo issues)

Parameters	Competencies	Indicators
	Ability to love, care, enjoy relationships Ability to communicate effectively	Examples of effective communication Appropriate eye contact Positive body language
	Listening and responding skills	Paraphrasing Frequency of open-ended, supportive questions
	Ability to have honest/ open communications	Recognition of unequal relationships and the reasons Examples of initiatives taken to repair relationships
	Ability to confront constructively, be assertive, negotiate, be open to other options, and resolve conflicts	Examples of conflicts resolved nonviolently Number of conflicts ignored or avoided
	Ability to build agreement Ability to respect other perspectives Ability to accept differences and move on Ability to recognize one's mistakes and change ones stance Ability to close relationships positively when required	Number of times I have confronted and advised someone else before listening with empathy, understanding the other person's perspective, and finding a solution together Number of times one has taken ownership for mistakes
B 2. Diversity/ inclusion	Ability to value differences Ability to connect with people from different backgrounds and abilities (cross-border relationships)	Number and quality of cross-border relationships Immediate peer group composition Celebrations of other cultures and festivals

(Annexure 6 Continued)

(Annexure 6 Continued)

Parameters	Competencies	Indicators
	Ability to influence other spaces to include others	Examples of actions that enhance social inclusion
B 3. Belonging	Effective membership in a group Ability to create or find and voluntarily join positive support groups Ability to trust and build trust	Ongoing membership in support groups Number of lasting relationships based on respect Frequency of commitments met Number of people who regularly confide in you
B 4. Consensus and collaboration	Ability to understand group dynamics and manage group processes Willingness to give and take, contribute, and be persuaded	Examples of successful group work Number of times you have held the group together by: inviting ideas, suggestions, participation; giving and accepting feedback; identifying, and responding to members needs; creating consensus and common vision Number of times violence used (verbal and emotional)

C. IMPACT ON SOCIETY

Parameters	Competencies	Indicators
C 1. Systems—thinking; intervening systemically (macro and micro levels) This will include the following attitudes: Sense of social responsibility/ social conscience	**Diagnose (preparation and analysis):** Ability to recognize, understand elements of a system	Listing and categorization of stakeholders Level and frequency of engagement with different stakeholders

Parameters	Competencies	Indicators
Commitment to future action/change	Knowledge and appreciation of community, environment, stakeholders and their needs, and available resources Ability to map interconnectedness of socioeconomic, political, cultural systems	Needs of stakeholders correctly identified and validated by them Frequency of correctly mapping connections and consequences Level of understanding of social challenges from a holistic perspective and my position in it
Deciding to make the change happen	Design (Planning): Ability to design appropriate interventions/ create a plan Ability to conceptualize appropriate interventions Ability to generate and analyze options and innovate where necessary (pros and cons) Ability to be inclusive and participatory Ability to communicate vision/mission	Knowledge of the issue and processes of systemic change Availability of a validated plan Frequency of demonstration of democratic values (e.g., building consensus, inviting participation) Articulation of SMART goals Accurate mapping of required resources and their availability Number of relevant, win-win solutions or options generated to address the issue Level of acceptance by peer groups and key stakeholders who have been adversely affected by the issue

(Annexure 6 Continued)

(Annexure 6 Continued)

Parameters	Competencies	Indicators
	Do/Act: ability to implement an intervention at levels of Self, immediate circle of influence, and beyond Ability to respond to a situation that demands action Ability to negotiate with relevant players and build agreement Ability to mobilize support and build a team Ability to build ownership for the process Ability to use resources effectively	Frequency of interventions at Self, immediate circle, and beyond Level of satisfaction of stakeholders (including Self) Level of satisfaction of stakeholders of processes adopted Frequency and level of participation in existing processes
	Evaluate: Ability to evaluate/assess the efficacy of intervention	Level of change that has occurred in the lives of the key stakeholders after the intervention Articulation of lessons learned Number of changes made based on lessons learned
	Ability to analyze yourself in the context of the social project	Articulation of how the issue and the intervention impact me

Annexure 7

The Vyaktitva Explorer

Like an iceberg (Figure A7.1), competencies lie above or below the waterline. Those that lie above the waterline and form the tip of the iceberg are most easily observed and acquired, such as technical skills and knowledge, whereas competencies that are submerged below the waterline are more difficult to observe and develop. These form the deeper level of the Self. We believe that leadership is not only the observable competencies but also the competencies of the deeper Self.

The Self is made up of the five elements (*tatvas*) of the universe: *(a)* Fire, *(b)* Sky, *(c)* Earth, *(d)* Water, and *(e)* Air. The sixth element, Vyakti, is an amalgamation of all five elements. Developed by Pravah and Vyaktitva, the Tatva framework is a tool to help you understand your

Figure A7.1: Iceberg Model

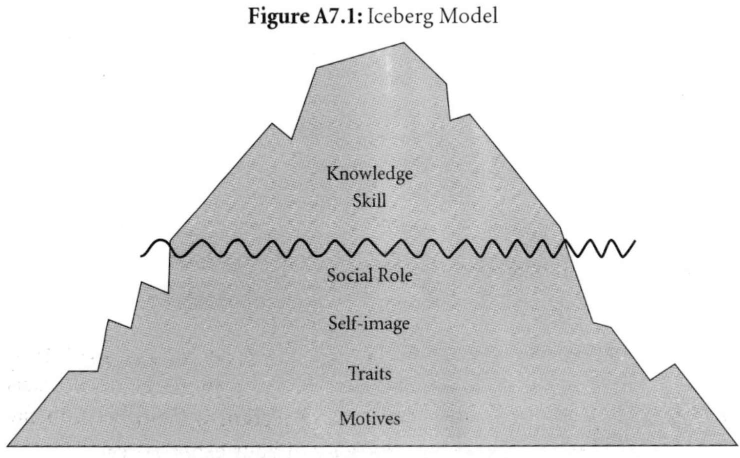

Source: http://www.luffalostale.eduoffices/ho/pepds/sf/tb.asp

vyaktitva (character) better. It helps you to map the different elements of your *vyaktitva* and the interrelationships between them, thus enabling you to identify points of potential change and self-transformation. The framework is based on the five *tatva*s of the universe, each of which symbolizes a different aspect of your character:

- Fire symbolizes warmth—EQ, teaming, relationships.
- Sky symbolizes the horizon—vision, goals, aspirations, desires, strategies.
- Earth symbolizes solidity—identity, structure, roles, boundaries, traits, habits, attitudes.
- Air symbolizes the atmosphere—values, assumptions, beliefs, mental models.
- Water symbolizes the flow—meta processes, such as systems thinking, creating and interpreting stories (which includes pattern recognition, choosing/judging wisely), deep self-awareness, building joyful community (which includes deep empathy, taking 100 percent responsibility/ownership, showing deep love and affection), and learnability.
- Vyakti is the amalgamation of all the five elements and for this instrument, we look at the external manifestation of the Vyakti. We call it Vyakti (external face). It is what is visible at the surface level and easily acquired, such as talents, skills, knowledge by an individual.

Each of the *tatva*s helps you to reflect on a different aspect of your Vyaktitva:

1. SKY—To what extent is my journey influenced by my destination?
2. EARTH—How well do I know myself?
3. AIR—How well informed is my worldview?
4. FIRE—How deeply do I relate to others in order to build a joyful community?
5. WATER—To what extent do meta processes enable my journey?
6. Vyakti (External face)—How well equipped am I to undertake this journey?

This tool will help you to reflect on your own *vyaktitva* and assess your personal transformation across time using facts about yourself. Facts help us recall our real experiences. This reflection will funnel into the final rating based on a collective summary of your experiences.

Figure A7.2: The Explorer Funnel

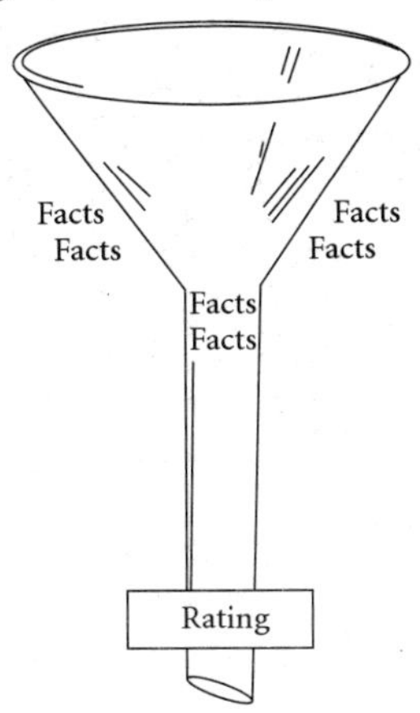

Source: Pravah.

Please fill in the facts in the following sheets for each of the *tatva*s, giving examples and numbers wherever you can, and then rate yourself on each of the *tatva*s using the following scale:

Ratings scale (1–6):

1. Not at all
2. To some degree
3. Quite a lot
4. To a large extent
5. Hugely
6. Totally

We request you to ask at least two other people who know you well—a colleague, a friend, a family member, or a supervisor/teacher—to fill up this form for you so that you can learn more about yourself through their eyes. Sharing this information may be difficult, but it builds trust and enables others to share too.

EXPLORING MY VYAKTITVA

S. To what extent is my journey influenced by my destination?

The destination gives a purpose to the journey. But it is the journey itself that needs to be foregrounded in our lives because that is what I can influence in the now.

Please pick and fill in at least **four** facts from the list below:

Indicators	Please give examples and numbers wherever possible
S I: Personal goals	
1. Do you have a primary purpose/vision in life? Please articulate.	
2. Number of specific and achievable goals I have set for myself in the last six months (as against other people's goals, such as parents, teachers). Examples.	
3. Number of goals in alignment/deviation from my primary purpose/vision.	
S II: My journey toward my goals	
4. Have I taken responsibility in the last six months for achieving goals in professional and personal spaces (e.g., family, friends, work, and others)?	
5. Examples of times I have revisited and changed my goals in the last six months. (This refers to how we adjust to emerging situations flexibly.)	
6. Number of times I have bounced back from failure and moved on constructively in the last six months.	
7. Examples of letting go of my own ambition in favor of the larger group's goal (group does not refer to oppressive group situations).	
Rating (1–6): To what extent is my journey influenced by my destination? Give reasons for the rating: 1. Not at all 2. To some degree 3. Quite a lot 4. To a large extent 5. Hugely 6. Completely without exception	

How well do I know myself?
Awareness of our deeper Self is critical for effective leadership and action in the outside world.
Please select and answer at least **five** facts from below:

Indicators	**Your response (please give examples as well as numbers wherever possible)**
E I: Self-awareness	
8. Percentage time in a day devoted to self-reflection	
9. Number of times I have been conscious of wearing a mask and not showing my authentic self in the last six months. (The assumption is that we all wear masks sometimes. The idea is not to promote wearing a mask but rather the awareness of it.)	
10. Number of times my assessment of my strengths and challenges has been different from others' perceptions (assuming you take frequent feedback from others)	
11. Number of times in the last six months that I have recognized that my behavior is emerging from a habit	
E II: Comfort with my Identities	
12. Number of times I have been flexible in moving between multiple identities (e.g., can I move between my identities as a boss and a friend?)	
13. Examples of questioning and negotiating given roles (family, religion, career, etc.) and finding creative, win-win alternatives	
E III: Self-esteem and Control	
14. Number of times I have taken ownership and apologized for my mistakes in the last six months	

15. Number of times I displayed my depression/anger in public in the last six months	
16. Examples of being assertive without being aggressive in the last six months	
17. Number of times I have been able to withstand peer pressure in the last six months	
Rating (1–6): How well do I know myself? Give reasons for the rating: Not at all To some degree Quite a lot To a large extent Hugely Completely without exception	

A. How well-informed is my worldview?
Our world view is informed by our values and stances developed after exploring and engaging with different perspectives.
Please select and answer at least **three** facts from below:

A I: Value recognition

Indicators	**Your response (please give examples as well as numbers wherever possible)**
18. Prioritize your top three values. How difficult was it for you to arrive at the top three values? How sure are you that this priority is the correct one?	
19. Number of perceptions you have changed in the last six months based on negative stereotypes you have recognized	
20. Number of times I have recognized where an opposing view point is coming from (the values behind it) and included it in my worldview	

A II: Living the Values without transgressing others' values	
21. Number of times I have taken an informed stance in the last six months based on a deep understanding of the issues (as against a mere opinion)	
22. Number of times I have changed my stance in the last six months based on new inputs	
23. Number of times I have chosen to decide/act in the last six months on the basis of prioritizing your values	
Rating (1–6): How well informed is my worldview? Give reasons for the rating: Not at all To some degree Quite a lot To a large extent Hugely Completely without exception	

F. How deeply do I relate with others to build a joyful community?
We cannot live like islands. Critical to leadership is the ability of taking people along in an authentic way.
Please select and fill in at least **five** facts from below:

Indicators (in the last six months)	Your response (please give examples as well as a number, wherever possible)
F I: Authentic relationships	
24. Number and quality of significant, lasting relationships carried over from the past.	
25. Number of times you have expressed feelings of love and affection appropriately	
26. Number of times in the last six months I have resorted to physical or emotional violence in a conflict	

27. Number of conflicts still unresolved	
28. Number of times you have taken full responsibility and inspired others to take full responsibility	
F II: Belonging	
29. Number of times you have sought assistance from others/a support group in the last six months	
30. Number of times you have confided in other people (joys and sorrows)	
31. Number of commitments made by you to others and not met in the last six months	
F III: Collaboration	
32. Number of times you have held the group (friends, colleagues) together in the last six months by	
i. identifying and responding to members' needs	
ii. inviting suggestions and participation	
iii. giving and accepting feedback	
iv. creating consensus and common vision	
v. inspiring others to step beyond role boundaries and take responsibility	
Rating (1–6): How deeply do you relate with others in order to build a joyful community? Give reasons for the rating: 1. Not at all 2. To some degree 3. Quite a lot 4. To a large extent 5. Hugely 6. Completely without exception	

W. To what extent do meta processes enable my journey?
Meta processes refer to a deeper level of the "How"—the way things get done. In contrast to skills that are easier to acquire, meta processes require a deeper transformation. They are the underlying currents in an ocean, whereas skills and talents are like the waves on the surface. Meta processes create the waves (e.g., skills cannot be internalized without appropriate attention to the learnability meta processes).
Please pick and answer a minimum of **seven** facts from below:

Indicators	**Your response (please give examples and numbers wherever possible)**
W I: Learnability	
33. Number of times I have identified my learning needs and developed a learning plan	
34. Number of times I have reviewed my learning plan and logged my insights about myself	
35. Number of times I have challenged myself and stepped out of my (physical and mental) comfort zone	
36. Number of times I have sought and responded to feedback in the last six months	
37. Number of significant, new attitudes, skills, and behaviors acquired in the last six months	
W II: Systems thinking	
38. Number of times I have engaged with stakeholders (that is, people contributing to and impacted by the issue) and correctly identified their needs in any intervention I make	
39. Number of times I have mapped the connections between the different stakeholders/systems and the consequences of my intervention	

40. Number of times I have recognized deeper patterns flowing in the system (e.g., a stomach ailment need not be attributable to what we eat but could also be related at a deeper level to stress)	
41. Number of times I have correctly diagnosed the most effective/leveraged point to initiate the intervention	
42. Number of times I have developed a plan and a budget for an intervention with specific goals and a resource mobilization strategy	
43. Number of relevant, win-win solutions generated to address the issue through an intervention	
44. Number of significant and lasting changes you have made at the levels of *(a)* Self, *(b)* your immediate circle, and *(c)* beyond	
45. Level of satisfaction of stakeholders (including yourself) with the outcomes achieved and processes adopted in the changes mentioned above	

W III: Interpreting and creating/narrating authentic stories (The access to yourself and the world is through stories. This meta process enables you to get to the real experience/story through facts rather than others' opinions.

46. When I hear a story, how many times have I … *(a)* asked questions not addressed in the story, *(b)* challenged the premise itself, *(c)* added value to understand the entire experience, *(d)* constructed meaning and related it to my own life?	
47. Percentage of times I have interpreted patterns correctly and judged the situation wisely (as close to the objective reality as possible)	

48. Number of authentic stories created/ narrated that are objective, without hidden agendas, relevant to the listener, anticipate questions, and give examples to help them understand better	
Rating (1–6): To what extent do meta processes enable my journey? Give reasons for the rating: 1. Not at all 2. To some degree 3. Quite a lot 4. To a large extent 5. Hugely 6. Completely without exception	

How well-equipped am I to undertake this journey?

Here we refer more to the surface level (waves) of *talents, skills, abilities, and knowledge* that we see in an individual in a transaction. These abilities have been well identified in many instruments and include strategic thinking, interpersonal skills, communication skills, planning, and project management skills, etc. While valuing these abilities, this instrument has focused on a deeper level of our character. However, we believe that it is important to answer the question mentioned above and rate oneself on this parameter.

Rating (1–6): How well equipped am I to undertake this journey? Give reasons for the rating: 1. Not at all 2. To some degree 3. Quite a lot 4. To a large extent 5. Hugely 6. Completely without exception	

RATING on a scale of 1–6

1. To what extent is my journey influenced by my destination? ☐
2. How well do I know myself? ☐
3. How well informed is my worldview? ☐
4. How deeply to I relate with others in order to build a joyful community? ☐
5. To what extent do meta processes enable my journey? ☐
6. How well equipped am I to undertake this journey? ☐

Welcome back! We hope it was an exciting journey, and you have come back with new insights about yourself.

How do you feel after going through this process?

Jot down some of the insights you have gained about yourself:

Before handing in your form, go through the following *checklist*, and ensure that you have:

- Filled up the minimum number of facts requested in the fact sheet?
- Given evidence in the form of examples and/or numbers for each of the facts filled in?
- Given a rating for each of the questions based on your reflection?
- Given reasons for the rating?

Bibliography

Altbach, Philip, G. 1970. "Student Politics and Higher Education," in *The Student Revolution: A Global Analysis*, pp. 99–119. Bombay: Lalvani Publishing House.

Arimpoor, J. 1983. *Indian Youth in Perspective—A Research Study*. Tirupattur: Department of Social Work, Sacred Heart College.

Arthur, James and Davies, Ian (eds). 2009. *Citizenship Education*, Vols 1–4. New Delhi: SAGE Publications.

Basu, Kaushik. 2007. "India's Demographic Dividend". Available at www.news.bbc.co.uk (downloaded on July 27, 2007).

Bhargava, M. and Dutta, K. 2005. *Women, Education & Politics—The Women's Movement and Delhi's Indraprastha College*. New Delhi: Oxford University Press.

Boggs, A. M. 2006. "A Matrix for Comparative Study of Student Movements: Twentieth Century Latin American, U.S. and Indian Student Movements," *Higher Education Perspectives*, 2 (2): 38–49.

Bose, M. 1982. *The Lost Hero*. London: Querte Book.

Carr, W. 2008. "Education for Citizenship," in James Arthur and Ian Davies (eds), *Citizenship Education, Vol. 1: Fundamental Issues—The Nature of Citizenship Education*. New Delhi: SAGE Publications.

Chandra, Prabodh. 1938. *Student Movement in India*. Lahore: All India Students Federation.

Chattopadhyay, G. 1987. "Bengal Students in Revolt against the Raj 1945–1946," in A. K. Gupta (ed.), *Myth and Reality: The Struggle for Freedom in India 1945–1947*. New Delhi: Manohar Publishers.

De Souza, P. R., Sanjay Kumar, and Sandeep Shastri. 2009. *Indian Youth in a Transforming World: Attitudes and Perceptions*. New Delhi: Centre for the Study of Developing Societies.

Eliot, T. S. 1962. "Little Gidding. Four Quartets." *The Complete Poems and Plays 1909—1950*. New York: Harcourt, Brace and World.

Etra, Alex. 2008. *Youth Development through Active Citizenship—Mapping Assets in South Asia. Working Document.* Washington D.C.: Innovations in Civic Participation.

Gandhi, M. K. 1947. "Students' Difficulties," in *Harijan*, Ahmedabad, August 7.

Hirschkind, Charles. 2011. "The Road to Tahrir," *Economic and Political Weekly*, XLVI (7): 13–15.

Jacob, K. S. 2010. "For More Humanity in Medicine," *The Hindu*, New Delhi, September 11, p. 10.

Jayaswal, R. 1992. *Modernization and Youth in India*. Jaipur: Rawat Publications.

Jeelani, Mehboob. 2011. "Reform School: Can the Youth Congress Expunge the Sins of Its Fathers Before It Inherits Their Wicked Ways?" *The Caravan: A Journal of Politics and Culture*, August 11.

Jeffs, T. and Smith, M. K. 1999. "The Problem of Youth for Youth Work," *Youth and Policy*, 62: 45–66. Available at http://www.infed.org/archives/youth.htm

Jhingan, Seema. 2010. "Foreign Education Bill—An Education Revolution in India or a Myth." Available at www.ezinearticles.com (downloaded on November 7, 2012).

Joshi, P. M. 1972. *Student Revolts in India: Story of Pre-Independence Youth Movement*. Mumbai: Sirur Printing Press.

Kabeer, N. 1994. *Reversed Realities: Gender Hierarchies in Development Thought*. New Delhi: Kali for Women.

Lochan, Kanjiv (ed.). 1996. *JNU: The Years. An Anthology by the Silver Memoir Committee*. New Delhi: Popular Prakashan.

Lukose, Ritty. 2005. "Consuming Globalization: Youth and Gender in Kerala, India," *Journal of Social History*, 38 (4): 915–993.

Mannheim, Karl. 1952. "The Problem of Generations," in Poul kocsverneti (ed.), *Essays on the Sociology of Knowledge*, pp. 276–320. New York: Oxford University Press.

Mathew, Liz. 2009. "The Lok Sabha has Become Older, but Is It Wiser Too?" *Mint*, April 13. Available at www.livemint.com

Matin, A. and Noor, Mohammad. 1995. *Indian Youth, Problems and Prospects*. New Delhi: Ashish Publishing House.

Mehta, P. 1971. *Indian Youth: Emerging Problems and Issues*. Bombay: Somaiya Publication.

Ministry of Labour and Employment. 2010. "National Skill Development Mission," PIB Press Release, Government of India, New Delhi. Available at http://pib.nic.in/newsite/erelease.aspx?relid=64862 (downloaded on November 8, 2012).

Moser, C. 1993. *Gender Planning and Development: Theory, Practice and Training*. London: Routledge.

Nair P. S., Murali Dhar, Vemuri, and Faujdar, Ram. 1989. *Indian Youth: A Profile*. New Delhi: International Institute for Population Sciences.

Nathaney, Dayo. 1946. *Karachi Students on the March: A Chronicle of Students' Movement in Karachi from 1905 up to the Present Day*. Mohan Panjabi for Hindustani Sahitya Astan.

NCERT. 2005. *The National Curriculum Framework*. New Delhi: NCERT.

Oxfam India. 2010. "Demanding Rights, Creating Opportunities—Oxfam India Strategy 2010–2015." Available at www.oxfamindia.org/resources

Patel, A. 2006. "A Framework for Integrating Youth Development in Community Development," unpublished paper for SRTT, Pravah, New Delhi.

Paul Choudhary, D. 1988. *Youth Participation and Development.* New Delhi: Atmaram and Sons.

Perold, Helene. 2009. *Nurturing Youth Active Citizenship in India: A Report on a Stakeholder Consultation.* Report submitted to Pravah and Innovations in Civic Participation, New Delhi.

Postman, Neil. 1994. *The Disappearance of Childhood.* New York: Vintage Books.

Pravah. 2009. "The Ocean in the Drop: A Perspective on Youth Ownership of Common Spaces," unpublished paper, Oxfam India.

Ray, N. R. et al. (eds). 1984. *Challenge: A Saga of India's Struggle for Freedom.* Chittagong Uprising Golden Jubillee Committee. New Delhi: People's Publishing House.

Sarkar, S. 1973. *The Swadeshi Movement.* New Delhi: People's Publishing House.

Sarswati, S. 1988. *Youth in India.* Indian Council of Social Sciences Research, New Delhi.

Schank, Roger C. et al. 1993–1994. "The Design of Goal-Based Scenarios," *The Journal of the Learning Sciences*, 3 (4): 305–345, Lawrence Erlbaum.

Shekhar, A. 2008. Unpublished Paper. *Reviving the 5th Space.*

Shokr, Ahmad. 2011. "The Price of Stability: Egypt's Democratic Uprising," *Economic and Political Weekly*, XLVI (7): 10–12.

Thakur, Atul. 2010. "Youngest Nation, Oldest Cabinet," *Sunday Times*, New Delhi, August 29, 2010.

Tendulkar, D. G. 1951. *Mahatma, Life of Mohandas Karamchand Gandhi,* Volume II. Vithalbhai K. Jhaveri and D. G. Tendulkar, Mumbai.

UN Economic and Social Commission for Asia and the Pacific. 2007. "Understanding Youth Issues in Selected Countries in the Asian and Pacific Region," p. 38. Available at http://www.unescap.org/publications

Upadhyay, Ashok. 2010. "Unrealised Demographic Dividend." Available at www.hindubusinessline.com (downloaded on November 4).

Varma, Ravindra. 1948. *Wither the Students' Movement or a Plea for the Establishment of a National Union of Students.* Published by Shri R. Bajaj, Bajajwadi on behalf of the All India Students' Congress, Wardha.

Varner, Stewart. 2007. "Youth Claiming Space—The Case of Pittsburgh's Mr. Roboto Project," in P. Hodkinson and W. Deike (eds), *Youth Cultures—Scenes, Subcultures and Tribes.* New York: Routledge.

Vishwa Yuvak Kendra. 1981. *For Youth in India: Schemes of the Central and State Governments.* New Delhi: Vishwa Yuvak Kendra.

World Development Report. 2006. *Development and the Next Generation.* World Bank Publications.

Index

"ABCED mindedness", 5
Active Citizenship, 30, 83, 119
  after Independence, 78–82
  and freedom movement, 66–73
  re-imagining of, 82–85
  as 5th Space, 65–66, 73 (*see also* 5th Space; freedom movement)
All India Catholic Universities Federation (AICUF), 79
anticorruption movement, 7–8, 24, 29, 43, 80. *see also* media
  and Independence movement, 67
Aristotle, 80, 83
Arnheim, Rudolf, 10
Association for Stimulating Know how (ASK), 130

Bengal Famine, students' response to, 68
Bharatiya Janata Yuva Morcha (BJYM), 41–42
Boorstein, Daniel, 8
border crossings, 86, 102–103
Bosco Institute, Guwahati, 50–51

cabinet, Indian, average age of, 22–24
Carr, Wilfred, 65
child/youthhood, concept of
  communication technology in, role of, 5–6
  creation of, 3–4
  disappearance of, 2
Chinnapan, 79
Christian Student movements, 40
citizen journalism, 87
classroom, concept of, need of change in, 6, 12
Communal riots 1946, student action during, 70
communication technology
  concept of youthhood and, 5–6
  effects of changes in, 5
    electronic media and, 7–11
    printing press and, 5–6
community development, youth contribution in, 38–39
community service, focus on, 39
community workers, 38
Commutiny, 122
Commutiny Media Network (CMN), 123
Confederation of Indian Industry (CII), 34
consumers, youth as, 33
contextual/generational influences on youth, 29
Continuous Comprehensive Evaluation scheme, by CBSE, 121
cybermohalla, 87

Democracy Connect, 41
demographic dividend, 33, 34, 61, 119
development stages of youth, 26–27, 28
Disappearance of Childhood (Neil Postman), 2

Doosra Dashak, Rajasthan, 49–50, 98
Drishti, 87

education
  and learning, 128
  in Middle Ages, 4
  purpose of, 34–35
  values and life skills, 120–121
electronic media, 6. *see also* anticorruption movement
  in 3rd space, 63
  role in closing generation gap, 7–11
Emile (Rousseau), 6
employment
  benefit of, 35
  creation and guarantee of, 61
extremists, young people use by, 43

facilitators
  need of, 99
  unbiased, 99
  youth, 117
family space, 60–61. *see also* freedom movement
5th Space, 65–66, 83–84, 90, 95–96. *see also* Active Citizenship; Pravah
  architecture of, principles in, 95–96
    charge of space, 98–99
    denizen's state of mind, 103
    fostering friendships and joyful engagement, 102–103
    measures for important elements, 100–101
    moving from known to unknown, 99–100
    organic renewal algorithm, 104
    ownership of space, 96–98
    present moment, focus on, 101–102
    promoting trust and safe hang out places, 102
    refl-action plan, 100
  reimagining of, 83–85
  social legitimization and promotion of, 118–125
  uniqueness of, 91–95
  and voyage from Self to Society and back, 92–95
  working process model for (*see* SMILE program)
freedom movement
  Active Citizenship and, 66–73
  governance after, 21, 24, 32, 78, 98, 129
  spaces encompassed in, 73, 78
    education and careers, 73–75
    family, 75–76
    friends, 76–77
    leisure and lifestyle, 77–78
  youth participation in, 19–20, 66–73, 85–87

generation gap, 1, 2
  creation of, role of print in, 3–6
  narrowing of, electronic media role in, 7–12
"Global Active Citizen", 80
global village, 11
G20 Meet, 22, 23
graphic revolution, 8
Grassroots Comics, 87
Green School Program, 42–43
gurukul system, 3

hanging out, 102
Hazare, Anna, 25, 68, 81
human capital, 37

identity formation stage, of youth, 46–47, 83
image revolution, 10
Independence movement. *see* freedom movement
India
  growth story, and statistics, 14–15
  as youngest nation, 18, 22, 23, 33
Indian Youth Congress (IYC), 41
Innis, Harold, 4, 7

Internet, 8–9, 11, 86, 89. *see also* electronic media
Inward Bound tents, 106–107

Jai Prakash Narain (JP) movement, 67, 79
Joyce, James, 5
juvenile crime rate, 2

knowledge gap, between adults and youth, 2, 5
knowledge monopoly, 2, 5, 12

Liberation Tigers of Tamil Eelam (LTTE), 44
Lok Sabha, age-wise representation in, 20

Maharashtra Yuva Manch (MYM), 51, 97
mall, attraction to, 62
Mannheim, Karl, 29, 58, 67
Manzil, New Delhi, 55–56, 104
Mead, Margaret, 1
media. *see also* electronic media
  public perceptions of youth by, 32
  role of, in participation of youth in movements, 72–73, 86–87
  use of, for promoting 5th Space, 122–123
Ministry of Youth Affairs, 24, 38, 123–125
Music For Harmony, 113
Must Bol, 123

Narmada Bachao Andolan, 43, 93, 96
National Association of Software and Services Companies (NASSCOM), 34
National Curriculum Framework 2005, for school education, 35
National Service Scheme (NSS), 38, 39, 81
National Skills Development Commission, 34
National Youth Policy 2003, 38–39, 124
Naxalite movement, 43
Nehru, Jawaharlal, 19
Nehru Yuva Kendra Sangathan (NYKS), 38, 39, 81
neoliberal decades, 24

ownership of space, 96–98
Oxfam India, 130

Pamuk, Orhan, 91
Patang, Sambaipur, 54–55
physical spaces, 89
political organizations, mobilization of youth by, 40–42
politics and governance, youth participation in, 19–24, 29–30
Postman, Neil, 2
Pravah, 46, 97, 130. *see also* 5th Space
  Change Looms program, 95
  re-imagining 5th Space at, 83
  SMILE program, 92
  Vyaktitva Explorer tool, 101, 111–112, 163–174
  youth-centric approach, 44, 46–47
  youth mobilization, for social change, 16–17, 43
printing press
  decline in, 6
  gap between adults and youth by, 5–6
  and origin of schooling, 3
public perceptions of youth, media role in, 32
PUKAR, Mumbai, 47–48, 97

Rajiv Gandhi National Institute for Youth Development (RGNIYD), 125
Rashtriya Swayamsevak Sangh (RSS), 40
religious organizations, mobilization of youth by, 39–40

SAHER, Mumbai, 51–52
school, 3
  creation of 5th Spaces within, 121
  future-orientedness of, 6
  gap between adults and youth by, creation of, 6
  impact of shifts in knowledge monopolies on, 12
  preparation for adulthood by, 5
  as product of printing press, 3
self-awareness workshop, 110–113
Self quest, 91
Shakha Milans, 40
Shanks, Roger, 91
Singh, Dinesh, 91
skill development programs, 34
SMILE alumni, 117
SMILE program, 105, 106
  action projects and youth facilitators, 116–117
  exposure visits and internships, 113–116
  Inward Bound interventions, 105–107
  tools used, 106–107
  Youth Addas, 107–113
    advocates, 113
    alchemists, 109
    catalysts, 109
    learners, 109–113
social change, youth as instruments of, 38–45, 81. *see also* 5th Space
  NGOs and social movements, 42–44
  political organizations, 40–42
  religious organizations, 39–40
  ways of youth engagement, 38
  youth ministry, 38–39
spaces, 58–59
  creation of, for young person, 46–47
  5th space, 65–66, 83–84 (*see also* Active Citizenship; 5th Space)
  socially sanctioned, for young people, 60, 64–65
  career or institution, 61
  friends, 63–64
  home, 60–61
  leisure and lifestyle, 61–63
Strategic Resource Group (SRG), 130
student and teacher, relationship between, 2
Student Christian Movement of India (SCMI), 40
Students Federation of India (SFI), 42
suicide bombing, 44

tabula rasa, 6
Thoughtshop Foundation, Kolkata, 52–54
TV, 2, 6, 7, 9–11, 86. *see also* electronic media; media

United States Agency for International Development (USAID), 36
US Department of Labor's Bureau of Labor Statistics, 9

value-based political leadership, 14, 19
vocational training, 34, 121
volunteering, for social change, 81
vote bank, 40, 44
Vyaktitva Explorer, 101, 111–112, 163–174

Women In Development (WID) approach, 36
women, in workforce, 36–37
women's development programs, 37, 38
workshops
  Conflict Positive, 109–110
  Get Real, 110–113

youth, 14, 16, 68
  age definition, 26
  as clients of development programs, 37
  diversity in age group of, 30
  economistic view of, 32–33, 34–37

engagement in social action,
research study on, 17–18, 129–130
findings of, 73, 149–154
indicative list of measures for component elements, 101, 155–162
list of informants, 131–132
methodology used, 130
objectives of, 129–130
octogenarians interviewed in, 147–148
Vyaktitva Explorer in, 111–112, 163–174
youth in forties who engaged in social action, 133–146
as instruments of social change, 38–45
involvement in policymaking, need of, 124
mobilization of, for social change, 16–17
participation of
decline in, 20, 21, 32
in freedom struggle, 19–20 (*see also* freedom movement)
in parliament, 19, 20
in politics and governance, 19–24, 29–30
role in governance after independence, 21, 24, 32, 78, 98, 129
traditions of sociology of, 26–27
developmental stages of youth, 28
Karl Mannheim's generational/context theory, 29
lifestyle choice and youth subculture, 28–29
transitions to adulthood, 27
viewing of, ways of, 33
Youth Addas, 107–113, 127
youth affairs, ministry for, 24–25
youth-centric development, 45–47, 56
organizations for, 47
Bosco Institute, Guwahati, 50–51
Doosra Dashak, Rajasthan, 49–50
Manzil, New Delhi, 55–56
Patang, Sambaipur, 54–55
PUKAR, Mumbai, 47–48
SAHER, Mumbai, 51–52
Thoughtshop Foundation, Kolkata, 52–54
YP Foundation, New Delhi, 48–49
YUVA, Mumbai, 51
Yuv Shakti, Ahmedabad, 52
youth clubs, 109
Youth Collective, 122–123
youth engagement cells, in organizations, 121–122
youth issues, neglect of, by political leadership, 24–25
Youth resource cells (YRCs), 52–54
youth strategy, by Rahul Gandhi, 41
youth subcultures, and life style choices, 27, 28–29
youth transitions, 26, 27
YP Foundation, New Delhi, 48–49
YUVA, Mumbai, 51
Yuv Shakti, Ahmedabad, 52

About the Authors

Ashraf Patel is a founder member and board member of Pravah and Commutiny—The Youth Collective. She is presently Director, Learning Voyages—Pravah and Organization Facilitator at Commutiny—The Youth Collective. From 1990 to 1994 she worked with SRF and Escorts Financial Services. After this stint with the corporate sector, Ashraf cofounded Pravah and was the chief executive from 1994 to 2001. She is also an Ashoka Fellow and has served on several working groups, including the Working Group for Youth and Adolescents set up by the Youth Ministry for the Eleventh Five Year Plan, the Working Group for Adolescent Education set up by the HRD Ministry for the Twelfth Five Year Plan, and the National Committee set up by the UNDP and the Youth Ministry for IYV+10. Ashraf did her bachelors in Physics from Delhi University followed by a postgraduate diploma in Industrial Relations Management from XLRL, Jamshedpur.

Meenu Venkateswaran is a founder member and board member of Pravah and Commutiny—The Youth Collective. At Pravah, she has worked in several capacities—including head of Teacher Training and as the CEO. Presently she is Director, Resource Mobilization and Partnerships at Pravah. She has also worked with MARG Marketing and Research Group, SRF Finance, and CRY, and has consulted with Ashoka-Innovators for the Public, Plan International, and Credibility Alliance. She is a trustee of Patang, a youth organization in Odisha and Spanda, a performing arts trust. Meenu completed her masters (1985) in Economics from Delhi School of Economics, Delhi University, and obtained a postgraduate Diploma in Management from Indian Institute of Management, Bangalore in 1990.

Kamini Prakash is presently a board member and Director, Research at Pravah. She also looks after Change Looms: A Learning and Leadership Journey—a program for young social entrepreneurs. She has worked as executive director, The Hope Project, Basti Hazrat Nizamuddin, New Delhi, and as a program associate, Urban Programs, Care India. She is also a board member of the Hope Project and the Fabindia School, Rajasthan. She obtained her masters in Social Policy and Planning in Developing Countries from London School of Economics, and her PhD in German Studies from Michigan State University, USA.

Arjun Shekhar is a founder member and board member of both Pravah and Commutiny—The Youth Collective. He is currently the President of the Pravah Board and director, Vyaktitva, a performance enhancement organization. He studied at the Delhi School of Economics, Delhi, and then XLRI, Jamshedpur. He worked at NIIT and SRF between 1990 and 1997. He is the author of the novel *A Flawed God* (2011).

Credits

Lead organization: Pravah

Partners: Oxfam India, Association for Stimulating Knowledge (ASK), Strategic Resource Group, Commutiny—The Youth Collective

Conceptualization: Arjun Shekhar, Ashraf Patel, and Meenu Venkateswaran

Writing: Arjun Shekhar, Meenu Venkateswaran, and Kamini Prakash

Research: Arjun Shekhar, Ashraf Patel, Bindiya Rawat, Kamini Prakash, Khilesh Chaturvedi, Meenu Venkateswaran, Ritikaa Khunnah, and Vartika Jaini

Illustrations: Smita Sen